Employability = Qualifications + Work Experience + Strategies x Contacts

$$E = Q + WE + S \times C$$

The

Graduate Jobs

Formula

HOW TO
LAND YOUR
DREAM CAREER

PAUL REDMOND

The Graduate Jobs Formula: How to land your dream career

This edition first published in 2010 by Trotman Publishing, a division of Crimson Publishing Ltd., Westminster House, Kew Road, Richmond, Surrey TW9 2ND

©Trotman 2010

Author Paul Redmond

British Library Cataloguing in Publication Data

A catalogue record for this book is available from the British Library

ISBN 978 184455 211 5

Printed and bound by Legoprint SpA, Trento

Contents

Contents

Contents

Figures
and tables

FIGURES

TABLES

Foreword

'Why write a book on the graduate job market?'

This was the question I was mulling over as I took the lift to the 33rd floor of the shining, steel and glass edifice at the heart of London's Canary Wharf. It was early September 2008 and I was on my way to give a guest lecture at one of the most prestigious investment banks in the world. The name of the firm? Lehman Brothers.

Two weeks later, I had my answer.

Ever since the dramatic fall of Lehman Brothers and the ensuing global economic crisis, the graduate job market has rarely been out of the news. Suddenly, everybody seems to want to talk about graduates – who they work for, how much they earn, what sort of jobs they do, and if going to university still represents value for money.

But there's a problem. Most of the existing books on the graduate job market were written 'BC' (Before the Crunch), a time when jobs were plentiful, the market was buoyant and graduates could more or less pick and choose who they worked for.

Like bankers' bonuses, those days are rapidly becoming a thing of the past. From here on in, it's 'AD' (After the Downturn) – a time of spiralling competition, under-employment and endemic risk. Because of this, much of the old career advice on how to get a graduate job seems slightly outdated and written for a by-gone era (even though that 'era' was less than two or three years ago).

Foreword

As a university careers professional, my work brings me into contact with many of the UK's leading graduate recruiters. I also work with students and graduates, helping them to explore their career options and formulate their plans. This dual perspective has given me a first-hand insight into the extent that graduate job markets are changing and the challenges that anyone who wants a graduate-level job can expect to face.

It is this dual perspective that I have tried to convey in this book – the first 'AD' careers guide written directly for students and graduates.

The information and advice contained in this book has been product-tested with employers, recruitment specialists and graduates. If applied carefully, it will give you a head-start on your competitors and an insight into how graduate recruiters think and behave. It will reveal to you the tactics needed to put together effective applications, give you ideas about how to succeed at assessment centres and interviews, and let you in on the secret of how to build your very own career network.

Remember, going to university is still the best career strategy there is, but only if you take positive steps to seize every opportunity you can find to boost your employability. Reading this book will show you how to do it. After all, it is *your* career we're talking about.

About the author

Dr Paul Redmond is one of the country's leading experts on graduate recruitment markets. An experienced writer, speaker and careers practitioner, Paul has presented at numerous events and symposia around the world and his articles have featured in most leading national newspapers. His research into generational theory, including the phenomenon of 'Generation Y' and 'helicopter parenting', has led to numerous appearances on TV and radio.

Paul's research brings him into contact with many leading graduate recruiters – many of whom he has spoken to during the course of writing this book.

In addition to being head of Careers and Employability at the University of Liverpool, Paul is an elected Fellow of the Royal Society of Arts, and Vice-President of the Association of Graduate Careers Advisory Services.

'An equation is something for eternity.'

Albert Einstein

Acknowledgements

For their ideas, encouragement and support I would like to thank my colleagues at the University of Liverpool, particularly those in the Careers and Employability Service. This is a fascinating time to work in graduate careers and I'm fortunate to work in such a supportive and stimulating environment.

Thanks also to the Association of Graduate Careers Advisory Services for giving me permission to use data from the 2010 edition of *What do Graduates do?* and to Martin Birchall at High Fliers. I would also like express my thanks to the many graduate recruiters whom I've worked with in the past few years, particularly all those who have so kindly and unreservedly shared with me their views and perspectives on the changing world of graduate recruitment. I hope I have been able to do justice to their opinions and views.

In particular, I would like to thank my editor, Alison Yates at Trotman Publishing, for her enthusiastic support for the book and for being a thoughtful and critical reader.

Finally, I would like to thank all my family for their support and encouragement. To them this book is dedicated.

"Most people are other people. Their thoughts are someone else's opinions, their lives a mimicry, their passions a quotation."

Oscar Wilde

Introduction

Get your career into gear

There is a famous scene in the 1994 film *Speed* in which two people – a cop (Keanu Reeves) and a member of the public (Sandra Bullock) – find themselves facing the terrifying prospect of having to navigate a speeding bus through the crowded streets of Los Angeles. Due to a convoluted storyline, the bus mustn't travel at anything less than 50mph – if it does, a bomb strapped to its undercarriage is primed to detonate. To make matters even more dramatic, neither has ever driven a bus before.

As the bus slaloms wildly through the traffic-packed streets, the drivers have no choice but to stick grimly to their task, dodging cars and keeping an ever watchful eye on the speedometer. Behind them, terrified passengers watch in horror, their fate no longer in their own hands.

Though undoubtedly far-fetched, this scene offers a useful metaphor to help you understand what life is like in today's over-heated, over-supplied graduate job market.

Think of it like this. Ahead of you is one of the most important decisions you'll ever have to make. It's not exactly life and death, but it will have a major impact on your future career – even if, as yet, you have no idea where that might be.

The choice is this: are you going to be a Driver or a Passenger?

While you're pondering, let me explain. If you choose to be a Driver, you're making a statement that you want to control your career; to put yourself in the driver's seat, to call the shots, make the decisions. It's your career, so it makes sense to you to be in charge of which direction you go. You do this in full awareness that along the way you're going to make a few mistakes, collide with a few fixed objects, run a few red lights. After all, as in the film, Drivers realise that they're going to have to learn as they go along. If you're a Driver, this is a price you're willing to pay.

> **If things seem under control you're not going fast enough.**
>
> Mario Andretti

Compared to being a Driver, life as a Passenger is a relatively sedentary affair. After all, you get to hog the back seat and watch someone else make all the decisions. All you have to do is show up and shut up. Best of all, you get the satisfaction of criticising the Driver when, inevitably, they make a mistake. Unfortunately, complaining is about all you can do. Because you don't take any risks, you rarely make mistakes, which means you don't have many chances to learn from them. Not only will you never get to know what it feels like to drive, you'll never have the satisfaction of knowing that any successes that you achieve along the way are down to you.

I'll let you into a secret. Most people are Passengers. Few people aspire to take their career destiny into their own hands. Instead, most are quite prepared to let others do it for them – friends, family, colleagues, managers, even the invisible hand of fate.

Drivers and Passengers

Today's world of work consists of Drivers and Passengers. Either you embrace change and try to do something about it, or you get out of the way and let the Drivers take control. Either way, being neutral isn't an option – you have to take sides. In today's job market not making a career decision is a career decision in itself.

Drivers are few and far between. But if your aim is to land a graduate job – a job for which a degree (or higher) is required, it's time to quit thinking like a Passenger and take the first few tentative steps in learning how to drive.

This book is a book for Drivers. Think of it as your ultimate Driver's handbook.

The 'war for talent'

If you are about to go to university or are shortly going to graduate, ahead of you lies the most competitive, challenging, exciting and ultimately daunting graduate job market of all time. Never before in the field of higher education have so many graduates, from so many universities, competed with each other for so few jobs. Never before have the rewards for those who succeed been so great, nor the risks for those who don't been so costly.

Not only are there more students graduating from university than any time in history, the on-going shockwaves from the recent credit crunch have led to a serious contraction in the number of jobs on offer. From this has emerged the biggest graduate bottle-neck of all time. Around 80 graduates are now competing for every graduate-entry job. In some sectors and for some careers, the ratio has already passed into the hundreds. This situation will only intensify.

The implications of this are enormous. Consider, for example, Microsoft. In 2009 the software giant received 15,000 applications for fewer than 150 graduate jobs. Not that this was particularly unusual: similar ratios were being reported that year by banks (yes, banks), accountants, lawyers, manufacturers, engineers and high-street retailers. In the past two years alone, applications to the NHS have rocketed by 83%, prompting an interesting question – do all these people really want to work in the health service, or is it a case of 'any hospital in a storm'?

An over-supply of graduates must, you might be forgiven for assuming, be extremely good news for employers. After all, Economics 101 states that over-supply must always represent good news for the consumer. Right?

Wrong. For employers, the surge in graduate job seekers is having the opposite effect. Rather than welcoming the deluge of applications, many say they are groaning under the strain. This is leading to a major shift in employers' attitudes to recruitment. So profound has this shift been that it's now possible to talk about recruitment markets 'BC' and 'AD' – 'Before the Crunch' and 'After the Downturn' (Table 1).

Table 1: Graduate job markets 'BC' and 'AD'

JOB MARKETS BC (BEFORE THE CRUNCH)	JOB MARKETS AD (AFTER THE DOWNTURN)
War for talent – graduates hold upper hand	War for talent – employers now calling the shots
Hundreds of mass recruitment events – careers fairs, milk round visits, on-campus presentations	Highly focused, small-scale events at a handful of selected institutions
Focus on recruiting students during their final year	Emphasis on recruiting students via one-year internships or sandwich placements
Rising annual graduate starting salaries	Salaries now tied to performance and ability
Firms allocate large budgets for attracting and recruiting graduates	Recruitment budgets across all sectors are slashed. Strong focus on value for money
Employers willing to accept 'average' applications	Only the most highly motivated now considered
Emphasis on transferable skills	Emphasis on qualifications, skills, work experience and networks (contacts)

In the job market BC employers were keen to welcome as many applications from students and graduates as they could attract. To raise their profile, many of them spent huge sums of money each year visiting university campuses and attending careers fairs. The fear, for many of them, was that they wouldn't recruit enough graduates – or that their new graduates would leave after one or two years, having been 'poached' by other firms. This now seems hard to imagine; but prior to the credit crunch 'retention' (keeping hold of your graduate recruits) was one of the biggest concerns facing graduate recruiters.

> ❝ Far too many students are applying for jobs without being able to demonstrate motivation or commitment; too many students and graduates are still submitting sub-standard applications in the belief that employers will interview them. ❞

Post-credit crunch, these fears suddenly seem overblown, the graduate job market is the equivalent of the Millennium Bug. It's a new world all of a sudden, and a new world order now applies. AD, that BC world now feels as distant as the Roman Empire. Graduate recruiters in their droves are turning their backs on large-scale recruitment activities.

While I was researching this book, I consulted a number of leading employers on the future of graduate employment. Each of them predicted that within the next three years their organisation would no longer be hiring graduates in the same way as in the past. For them, the days of visiting numerous campuses and of hiring stalls at careers fairs were coming to an end. Not only was it expensive, it was highly inefficient. As one recruiter said:

> ❝ Who wants to visit dozens of university careers fairs when you can attract all the graduates you need on-line and at a fraction of the cost? ❞
>
> Graduate Recruiter

The graduate job market 'AD' has also witnessed a shift in the balance of power away from graduates and towards employers (see Table 1).

This is having a profound impact on the relationship between recruiters and students. Unfortunately, however, for many students the new AD reality hasn't sunk in. Far too many students are applying for jobs without being able to demonstrate motivation or commitment; too many students and graduates are still submitting sub-standard applications in the belief that employers will interview them. But, as this book will show, they won't. As one recruiter said:

> ❝ Last year was a bad year for us: too many poor quality applications and too many people applying to us without knowing why. We won't be going through that again. ❞

Graduate recruiter

Poor quality applications? People applying for jobs without knowing why? Don't these students know there's a war on?

No longer a phoney war

For much of the past decade graduate recruiters have been locked in an increasingly desperate 'war for talent'. The consequences of this 'war' are financial. Every year, graduate recruiters spend on average £80,000 on recruitment. Larger firms spend considerably more.

> ❝ It's the 'war for talent', and like it or not, you're about to be conscripted. ❞

According to research by the Association of Graduate Recruiters (AGR), hiring graduates now costs some firms over £500,000 a year. Not surprisingly, if a company has spent this much to hire you, they expect you to be good.

The second factor behind the war for talent was a perception, shared by many graduate recruiters, that while there might be more graduates on the market, the actual amount of 'talent' was finite. In other words, just because there are more graduates on the market, employers don't necessarily believe they are all necessarily of equal quality. More doesn't exactly equate to less; but at the same time few employers buy the idea that more graduates means more talent!

The idea of the 'war for talent' – and, more importantly, what it means for your career – is explored in Section 1.

The quest for employability

For the past five years I have been on a quest – a quest to discover the secret of employability.

Much has been written about employability: what it means, who it applies to, what its limitations are. Much of this literature (including my own) was written primarily for academics and careers practitioners. How it might be used profitably by students and graduates was never very clear. To me, this always seemed like a wasted opportunity. Instead of being used as a resource for academic dissertations, why couldn't research on employability also help students as they prepared for job interviews and assessment centres?

So the last thing I wanted to do was write another academic paper. I wanted instead to find a bridge between academic research and a practical guide to the job market for students and graduates.

For the past five years I have been working with a wide range of employers and recruiters to find out what they really want from graduates (ie going beyond what employers write on their websites and in their recruitment brochures). From these consultations several points soon emerged.

In all organisations, the value of a degree qualification remained the same, despite the rapid growth of student numbers. But there was a catch. The increase in student numbers meant that a degree, however brilliant, was no longer enough. Employers in all sectors told me that they wanted their graduates to have *more*. More skills, more drive, more commitment, more commercial awareness, more relevance to their organisations.

The problem was how to measure this. How can any employer know, within the strictures of the formal recruitment process, whether the politely spoken person sitting opposite them will gel with their clients while at the same time not disgracing themselves at the office party?

Interviews and assessment centres – though costly and time consuming – will get you only so far. References and personal testimonies are practically useless. Ultimately, employers told me that the decision to hire often comes down to other factors. Some of these factors are visible and transparent; others are not.

Uncovering these factors became the focal point of my research. Ahead of me lay the prospect of writing more academic papers – few of which, I realised, would be read by the very people who stood the best chance of benefiting from the work: students and graduates. So I decided to take a different line. Instead of writing an academic study, I would try to condense my theory of employability into a very brief, very concise formula.

The formula for employability

Using a formula to reveal the secret of employability might appear slightly strange – like using a formula to prescribe what it takes to find an ideal partner, or how to win *The X Factor*. For most of us, apart from a couple of largely forgotten years spent studying Maths GCSE, looking at the world through the prism of a formula is not something we're used to.

But a formula has one major advantage: it's extremely useful when trying to summarise or relate complex theories. Consider, for example, the most famous formula of all time, Einstein's formula for relativity.

Albert Einstein was probably the greatest physicist the world has ever known, and the theory of relativity was the pinnacle of his life's work. Einstein's theory of relativity explored many difficult problems that had been challenging physics for centuries, including what would happen to our view of the world if we could travel very fast.

For Einstein, 'very fast' meant somewhat faster than 50mph. In fact, it meant travelling at 186,000 miles per second – the speed of light. In summing up his theory, Einstein developed a formula: $E = MC^2$. As he later said:

" Equations are more important to me, because politics are for the present, but an equation is something for eternity. **"**

Albert Einstein

Devising a formula for employability

To help you acquire the skills, knowledge and insights you'll need to operate in the new graduate job market, this book provides you with a unique formula for how to become not just employed, but *employable*. Once you've grasped it, it will give you with a powerful insight into today's graduate recruitment market – what employers are looking for, what makes successful candidates stand out from all the rest, and how you can convince employers that you have what it takes.

This formula has another advantage: it's incredibly short. In today's world, brevity matters. Few of us have the time to read lengthy publications and papers on employability. What's needed is a formula – one that can be easily memorised.

This formula is so short in fact that you can 'tweet' it to your friends and still have 130 characters left.

So now, the time has come to unveil the formula for graduate employability:

$$E = Q + WE + S \times C$$

Six letters and four symbols: the alpha and omega of graduate employability. All you need to know about how to make yourself indispensable to employers – and not a textbook or academic journal in sight!

Each of the letters **E, Q, WE, S, C** stands for an essential stage in the process of making you employable – the essential nuts and bolts of what it takes for you to master your own career. If we were to write out the formula in longhand it would read:

> **" Employability equals Qualifications plus Work Experience plus Strategies multiplied by Contacts. "**

In other words, the formula means that for you to become employable you will need to make sure that you possess the right *qualifications*, relevant and up-to-date *work experience*, *strategies* that employers value and want to hire and, most of all, a group of proactive and appropriately placed *contacts*.

How this book works

The Graduate Jobs Formula has been designed so that you can browse any chapter you like in any order you like. You can, of course, also read it sequentially.

To illuminate the text, quotes from graduate recruiters and past graduates are included. For most of these, personal and company names have been omitted. There is a good reason for this. Like all professionals, recruiters are more likely to speak openly if they know that they and their organisations will not be directly identified. The alternative is to resort to the safe but bland marketing jargon put out by corporate communications departments.

That said, job roles and company sectors have been identified in order for you to get a flavour of how people from different sectors and industries view graduate recruitment.

So that you can explore each of the five components of the formula, the book is divided into five sections, each of which takes an element of the formula and gives you lots of ideas, tips and examples for developing your employability in this area. The following paragraphs give you a brief overview of the five sections.

E = Employability (Section 1)

The first section looks at what it means to be 'employable' and how this differs from being 'employed'. Also covered here are what a 'graduate' job means, what graduates do after university and what employers really want from applicants. The section also looks at universities, exploring why employers target some institutions and not others with their vacancies, and looking at the different categories of universities. It concludes by taking a look at graduate starting salaries.

Q = Qualifications (Section 2)

Section 2 takes a closer look at university degree courses and the types of careers that some of the most popular academic subjects can lead to. It uncovers the details of how different subjects compare with each other and reveals what graduates from various subject clusters do within the first six months of graduation.

WE = Work Experience (Section 3)

Section 3 explains why work experience is rapidly becoming a prized graduate *commodity* – one that can be bought and sold in the job market. The value of this commodity, like that of gold or share prices, rises and falls with prevailing economic conditions. As George Orwell might have said, all work experience is equal, but some work experience is definitely more equal than others.

S = Strategies (Section 4)

If you are to avoid becoming yet another casualty of today's Weapons of Mass Rejection, you need the strategies to be able to compete at the highest level – the skills to write effective applications and CVs, and the skills to make a powerful impact when meeting with employers – either in interviews or in assessment centres.

Having the right strategies is essential when the competition for graduate job is as intense as it is today.

C = Contacts (Section 5)

Contacts are the final part of the graduate employability formula. Without contacts, you have no choice but to join the queue, to hope and pray that one day your number finally comes up and that you will somehow be in the right place at the right time. The trouble is, it won't. Without contacts you are always the last one to know, the last one to apply, the last one to hear about that fantastic new opportunity. Worse, without contacts, employers look on you as an outsider – a risk. That is why the formula doesn't just add contacts to qualifications, work experience and skills – *it is multiplied by them.*

Most careers books tend to steer clear of discussing the power of contacts. Writers become nervous that it can so easily be interpreted as preaching nepotism. But who you know and, more importantly, who knows you, is essential when applying for jobs. This isn't to imply that knowing the right people will mean you don't have to play by the rules or can cut corners – which you definitely can't. But cultivating contacts will help you to gain access to new networks from which you will gain important insights and information – information that can be very effective when applying for jobs.

But don't think you have to be born into the right families or have gone to the 'right' schools to gain powerful contacts. As this book will show, the leads that you need are literally a phone call, a conversation or an email away. All you need to do is identify a spare 20 minutes, and you can begin building your own network. Section 5 shows you how and where to begin networking

E = Employability,
Q = Qualifications,
WE = Work Experience,
S = Strategies and
C = Contacts

$$E = Q + WE + S \times C$$

"I never think of the future. It comes soon enough."

Albert Einstein

Chapter 1

The meaning of employability

To be employable means that you are less dependent on the vagaries of the market and more capable of looking after your own career.

The quest for employability

As quests go, the quest for employability remains one of the most enduring and elusive in the world of higher education. Countless books, magazine articles, academic journals and research papers have been published on the subject, each with the same noble aim – to decode the Secret of Employability.

Why employability should continue to remain so maddeningly elusive for most people can be partly explained by the number: 2,640,000.

In March 2010, there were 2,640,000 entries on Google for the word 'employability'. If you were to read just one of these entries every day for the rest of your life, you would need 7,200 years to plough through them. Or you can just read this book.

As most people are unwilling to spend even seven *minutes* reading articles on employability, it's no surprise that most of the collected wisdom on the subject, like the location of the fabled city of Atlantis, remains lost.

So what does it mean to be 'employable'?

A brief history of employability

'Employability' is one of those words that turn grammatical purists purple. I should know. Once, while being interviewed on a radio talk-show, the host took me to task for using the 'E' word. *'Employability* – that's not a real word,' she fumed. Apparently she thought I'd just invented it.

I hadn't. Employability is a word with a long history; a word that is receiving increasing amounts of air time.

The meaning of employability

To be employed is to be at risk; to be employable is to be secure. This means that having a job isn't enough. You need to be able to generate new opportunities, new openings, and new possibilities. This is what it means to be employable.

The origins of the word 'employability' can be traced back to the First World War, when the issue of how to resettle huge numbers of ex-servicemen back into the labour market dominated public debates. 'Employability' circa 1918 meant helping ex-soldiers to acquire the skills and the ability to find and maintain employment, often against a backdrop of harsh social and economic circumstances.

Zoom forward a century, and although the social and economic landscape has completely changed, the actual meaning of the word 'employability' remains much the same. Only now the focus isn't on ex-soldiers, but on graduates.

Of the UK's 2.4 million students:

- The majority (56%) are female
- 16% are from ethnic minorities
- 6.6% have a registered disability
- Six out of 10 will gain a first or an upper second class degree
- 53% will work during term time
- Most will graduate with average debts totalling £10,500

Employability redux

Despite its political prominence, no single, undisputed definition of the word 'employability' has ever been agreed. But between the different definitions that you will encounter, certain themes tend to reoccur. The most common of these is *self-sufficiency*.

As economists have long recognised, employment isn't all that it's cracked up to be. For a start, it's notoriously unreliable. As economies change, so do patterns of employment. When market conditions are good, jobs grow and flourish; when they diminish, jobs are lost.

Technology also wreaks havoc on the job market. The launch of the high-street cash machine led to the loss of thousands of banking jobs. The personal computer had a similar impact on office jobs.

This is where *employability* has a distinct advantage. To be employable means that you are less dependent on the vagaries of the market and more capable of looking after your own career. How? Because to be employable means that you have all the qualifications, work experience, strategies and contacts necessary to take control of your own destiny. You're a Driver, not a Passenger.

Being able to drive, in a career sense, is one of the big ideas underpinning employability, one of the ways that you can differentiate it from employment. There are other differences between the two terms (Table 2).

Table 2: The differences between employment and employability

TO BE IN EMPLOYMENT	TO BE EMPLOYABLE
Job	Career
Contract	Contacts
Job description	Career objectives
9–5	24/7
What you know	Who you know
Dependent on previous qualifications	Constant retraining
Managed	Developed
Works *for* ...	Works *with* ...
Local view	Global view
TGI Friday!	TGI Monday!

To be *employed* means that ultimately you are dependent on a range of extraneous factors, eg the profitability of your employer, the actions of shareholders, where you live, even what your boss thinks of you. Many of these factors are beyond your control. After all, no matter how hard you work, if your company goes bust, your job will vanish. Brutal perhaps, but true.

Employability, on the other hand, turns employment on its head. Being employable doesn't mean that you are immune to economic conditions, but it does mean that you are in the driving seat. According to Professor Mantz Yorke, 'employability' refers to a set of achievements which, taken together, 'constitute a necessary but not necessarily sufficient condition for gaining employment'.

> ❝ Employability means more than being employed: it implies the ability to be self-sufficient, to be able to create your own opportunities ... to be able to stand on your own feet and be the CEO of 'Me plc' ❞.

But it doesn't come easily. Employability is like physical fitness: you have to keep plugging away, constantly looking to raise your game. If being employed is all about securing a job, being 'employable' is about perfecting a process – the process of constantly improving your qualifications, strategies, work experience and contacts.

Definitions of employability

'[Employability means] a set of skills, knowledge and personal attributes that make an individual more likely to secure and be successful in their chosen occupation(s) to the benefit of themselves, the workforce, the community and the economy.'
Higher Education Academy, 2006

'A set of attributes, skills and knowledge that all labour market participants should possess to ensure they have the capability of being effective in the workplace – to the benefit of themselves, their employer and the wider economy'.
CBI, Employability and Work Experience

E = Employability

So what are the skills which, according to employers, will make you employable?

In the report 'Future Fit: preparing graduates for the world of work', the CBI set out a list of employability-related skills.

- **Self-management:** readiness to accept responsibility, flexibility, resilience, self-starting, appropriate assertiveness, time management, readiness to improve own performance based on feedback/reflective learning.

- **Team working:** respecting others, co-operating, negotiating/persuading, contributing to discussions, and awareness of interdependence with others.

- **Business and customer awareness:** basic understanding of the key drivers for business success, including the importance of innovation and taking calculated risks – and the need to provide customer satisfaction and build customer loyalty.

- **Problem solving:** analysing facts and situations and applying creative thinking to develop appropriate solutions.

- **Communication and literacy:** application of literacy, ability to produce clear, structured written work and oral literacy – including listening and questioning.

- **Application of numeracy:** manipulation of numbers, general mathematical awareness and its application in practical contexts (eg measuring, weighing, estimating and applying formulae).

- **Application of information technology:** basic IT skills, including familiarity with word processing, spreadsheets, file management and use of internet search engines.

Underpinning each of these attributes, according to the CBI, the 'key foundation' should be 'a positive attitude: a "can-do" approach, a readiness to take part and contribute, openness to new ideas and a drive to make these happen'.

But even this is not enough to guarantee employability. Entrepreneurship, or a sense of enterprise, is also required – or as the CBI terms it, 'an ability to demonstrate an innovative approach, creativity, collaboration and risk taking'.

All this might sound like hard work. And it is. That's why so many people have only one career strategy: to get a job and cling on to it for dear life. Employers have a name for these people. They call them 'The Living Dead'.

Under-employment: the return of the living dead

If employability is something you have never thought about, you're not alone. Most people spend more time every year planning their summer holidays than their careers. Unfortunately, judging by the number of people who are chronically unhappy in their jobs, it shows.

Believe it or not, for today's graduates, the biggest threat on the career horizon isn't unemployment; it's under-employment.

- While at work, 33% have taken class A and B drugs
- 20% of US workers has had sex with a co-worker
- 70% of internet porn sites are accessed during the working day
- 30% of midweek visitors to a major UK theme park admits to being on the sick
- UK doctors receive 9m 'suspect' requests for sick notes every year
- 14.6% of UK office workers say they surf the web constantly

Extract from 'The Living Dead', by David Bolchover (2005)

For one writer, such people are the new 'living dead' – employees who have become so disengaged and disillusioned with their jobs that they spend months and even years sitting in offices doing next to nothing – talents wasted, skills long forgotten.

Avoiding 'living dead' jobs is one of the principle reasons why learning to become employable is so important. For today's generation of students, the risk of finding yourself in a job for which you are either over-qualified or over-skilled is an ever-present possibility. Unfortunately, the results can be both career and life-damaging.

Employability or 'graduate' job?

But before we finish with employability, there is one more important point to make. Being employable doesn't necessarily mean a ticket to a 'graduate' job; it means being flexible, being able to think outside of the box; having the guts to do things differently – even if it means shocking people so much that you find yourself in a national newspaper.

This is exactly what happened to a graduate called Nicola Gillison.

Case study: Plumbergate

 Oxford Graduate Quits City Job to Retrain as Plumber "

Headline, *Sunday Telegraph*, 19 January 2003

Apologies to Jane Austen, but it is a truth universally acknowledged that a graduate in possession of a good degree must want to work for a leading graduate recruiter. Or is it?

At least that's how it must have seemed when Nicola Gillison graduated with a degree in French from Lady Margaret Hall, Oxford and was snapped up by a smart City accountancy firm. But even high-flying careers cannot avoid the odd spot of turbulence and after two stressful years, Nicola realised that life in the City pressure-cooker wasn't for her. She resigned, and meditated long and hard on what to do next. Her decision, when it came, took everyone by surprise. She decided to become a plumber.

Designer suit to boiler suit

Few graduate career decisions taken in recent years have caused as much controversy as Nicola's. 'Plumbergate' even made the national newspapers. By trading her designer suit for a boiler suit, Nicola did for the graduate job market what the iPod did to the recording industry. She turned it on its head.

But why should the story of a modern languages graduate quitting her job as an accountant to retrain as a plumber be considered newsworthy? Who says Oxford graduates shouldn't be plumbers? Who says women graduates shouldn't be plumbers? After all, plumbing offers numerous career advantages, of which self-employment, flexible working hours and competitive pay are but a few. (According to one survey the average plumber takes home £80,000 a year – considerably more than most graduate salaries.) As career choices go, it's also relatively secure. Compared to City jobs, plumbers are probably better insulated against economic downturns.

Perhaps the real reason why Nicola captured the attention of the national newspapers is more prosaic. Despite the enormous changes that have taken place over the past few decades in work and higher education, Oxford graduates are just not expected to work as *plumbers*. Women, maybe; Oxford graduates ... come on!

The news coverage surrounding Nicola's career change illustrates an important fact about the graduate job market: it remains dominated by traditional thinking. Even today, after almost two decades of massive economic, cultural, social and global shifts, ideas of what constitutes an appropriate (or, even more so, inappropriate) job for a graduate to do continue to inform debates on higher education.

The problem is, as Nicola demonstrated, many of these ideas are out of date.

All change

The idea that graduates don't work as plumbers, or nurses, or care assistants, or start their own businesses is only one of the many misconceptions which continue to surround the graduate job market.

The fact is, in today's job market, change has occurred so quickly that much of the old thinking about what constitutes 'appropriate' and 'inappropriate' jobs for those with university degrees has failed to keep up. Partly, this is down to history. Less than a century ago Britain was a manufacturing nation, the engine room of the global economy. From its factories came millions of three-dimensional products made of iron and steel; things that lasted for a lifetime; things you could drop on your foot.

Britain's changing job scene

In today's Britain, heavy engineering employs barely a third of the total number of people who make their living working in Indian restaurants. Few of those eating in these restaurants will be employed in jobs which existed as recently as 1980. Britain now has three-times more PR consultants than coal-miners and 10 times more computing analysts than chimney sweeps. The speed of change is now so rapid that the 10 most popular careers in 2010 did not exist ... in 2004.

All this proves that any discussion about what graduates do has to be contextualised against a backdrop of transformative social, economic and historical change. Blue-collar or white-collar; office job or home worker — in today's world of work, who cares?

As W.B. Yeats wrote, *'all changed, changed utterly'*.

Chapter 2

Re-imagining the graduate job market

When advertising their vacancies, roughly seven out of 10 graduate recruiters ask for 'any' degree subject. Students often find this confusing. How can your degree subject – for three or four years the focal point of your studies – be so easily overlooked by employers?

T his chapter looks at the changing relationship between universities and graduate careers. It also challenges many of the common assumptions about 'graduate' jobs. In particular, five key issues will be explored:

- What is a 'graduate' job?
- Why do employers want graduates?
- Who employs graduates – and what do they look for?
- What is the graduate job market?
- Do employers prefer some universities over others?

Defining the 'graduate' job

As we have seen, the question of what is and isn't a graduate job remains hotly debated. On one side are those who claim that 'graduate' jobs are any jobs carried out by graduates. Opposing them are those who argue that this view conveniently overlooks the kinds of changes discussed in Chapter 1. For them, 'graduate' jobs are still identifiable – even if spotting them is far more complicated than in the past. Supporters of this view have also come to accept in recent

> " We are in graduate recruitment for the long term, and it will continue so that we can meet our goal – which is to have the right skills and capabilities in the organisation to meet the energy gap of the future. "
>
> Bob Athwal, Head of Graduate Schemes, RWE npower

years that as the competition for 'graduate' jobs intensifies, it is inevitable that a growing number of graduates will be employed in 'sub-graduate', or 'non-graduate' jobs.

The origins of the debate over what is and what-isn't a 'graduate' job gathered pace in the mid-1990s, when numbers of students enrolling in higher education started to expand. Prior to that, it was widely assumed that 'graduate' jobs were jobs that were generally clustered around a handful of old professions. Typically, these included law, medicine, teaching and the civil service. As we have seen, today things are seldom as clear cut.

Once the IT revolution got under way, such tidy distinctions soon began to break down. Suddenly, from Silicon Valley, emerged new and strange sounding job titles: *consultant, C++ programmer*. None of these lent themselves to easy classification. Matters weren't helped by the fact that Bill Gates and Steve Jobs – the Fidel Castro and Che Guevara of the IT revolution – were themselves non–graduates. Instead, both had dropped out of their university courses without bothering to stick around to finish their degrees (not that this prevented universities around the world from queuing up to offer them honorary ones).

Alongside the IT revolution, other changes were taking place. Deregulation of financial markets saw a massive increase in the numbers of jobs in banking, accountancy, insurance and investment banking. As the number of jobs in manufacturing and industry declined, jobs in business services first doubled, then trebled. Britain's days of being the workshop of the world were over. From now on, it would be its broker, banker, tax adviser and advertising agency. All of these jobs required graduates – thousands of them.

For national governments, this explosion of new jobs created a problem. If no one was sure any longer whether or not a job was at graduate level, how could they be sure that graduates were still entering jobs that were commensurate with their skills and education?

Peter Elias and Kate Purcell from the Warwick Institute for Employment Research (IER) analysed the changing structure of the labour market and in particular, the kinds of jobs graduates were employed in. They found that jobs where graduates had been targeted invariably required at least one (and normally more than one) of the following factors:

- Expertise and knowledge deriving directly from higher education
- The ability to play strategic or managerial roles
- High-level interactive skills

Analysing data from recent graduate surveys they conducted, they found that graduates in jobs that fell into traditional categories of graduate employment (e.g. doctors, solicitors and teachers) tended more often to report that they were required to use their 'graduate expertise'. Those in newer areas of graduate employment (e.g. marketing and sales managers, management accountants, and probation officers) were more often in jobs that had a significant strategic or managerial element where the transferable skills they had learned were more important than their 'graduate expertise'.

Elias and Purcell then set about creating a matrix against which to measure 'graduate' employment. Table 3 illustrates this matrix. Five categories of graduate jobs are proposed: 'traditional' graduate occupations (e.g. doctors, solicitors, teachers and scientists); 'modern' graduate occupations (e.g. programmers, writers, primary school teachers and managers); 'new' graduate occupations (e.g. marketing, physiotherapists, designers); 'niche' graduate occupations (e.g. midwives, nurses, sports professionals); and 'non-graduate' occupations.

Elias and Purcell's matrix offers a useful way of understanding how opportunities for graduates are changing. In their latest analysis (2009) they show how the profile of the occupational structure has been shifting towards more highly-skilled and away from unskilled occupations, where the proportions of all their 'graduate' categories increased substantially relative to the increase in non-graduate jobs between the early 1990s and 2008/9. There has been remarkably little change during this period in the proportion of employees employed in lower and unskilled categories, while the proportion of the workforce

Table 3: The new categories of graduate employment
Source: Elias and Purcell 2004:61

TYPE OF JOB	CONTEXT	EXAMPLE OCCUPATIONS
Traditional graduate occupations	The established professions, for which, historically, the normal route has been via an undergraduate degree programme	Solicitors, medical practitioners, HE and secondary education teachers, biological scientists/biochemists
Modern graduate occupations	The newer professions, particularly in management, IT and creative vocational areas, which graduates have been entering since educational expansion in the 1960s	Directors, chief executives, & software professionals, primary school teachers, authors/ writers/ journalists
New graduate occupations	Areas of employment, many in new or expanding occupations, where the route into the professional area has recently changed such that it is now via an undergraduate degree programme	Marketing & sales managers, physiotherapists, occupational therapists, management accountants, welfare, probation officers, countryside/park rangers
Niche graduate occupations	Occupations where the majority of incumbents are not graduates, but within which there are stable or growing specialist *niches* which require higher education skills and knowledge	Leisure and sports managers, hotel/ accommodation managers, nurses, midwives, retail managers
Non-graduate occupations	Graduates are also found in jobs that are likely to constitute under-utilization of their higher education skills and knowledge.	*Sales assistants, Filing and record clerks, Routine laboratory testers, Debt, rent and cash collectors*

in professional, managerial and technical occupations has grown steadily and is expected to continue to grow in the next decade, despite short-term fluctuations in demand for particular occupations as a result of the recession.

All this further illustrates the redundancy of the blue and white collar debate while showing just how rapidly the job market for graduates is evolving. For students about to plan their future, the sheer speed of change raises numerous issues.

Why employers hire graduates

There are several reasons why employers hire graduates. Research shows that graduates offer higher-level skills and knowledge; they also come with added qualities such as the capacity to learn quickly and to be able to process lots of information. But employers also view some graduates as future managers – the people who will one day run their organisations. This makes them very choosy about who they recruit. So choosy that they have developed

> " Few recruiters ask for specific degree subjects. 70 per cent of firms ask for applicants from 'any' degree subject. "

a range of complex sifting procedures designed to weed out all but the best applicants. In a report by the *Graduate Recruitment Bureau*, entitled '*The Seven Benefits of Hiring Graduates*', employers listed several reasons why companies recruit graduates. Although the article was written for employers, it's useful to look at employers' reasons for hiring graduates.

The benefits of hiring graduates – an employer's perspective

Affordable
Graduates earn lower salaries than experienced hires but have huge potential. Average graduate salaries are currently £21,000.

Proven return on investment
Their ideas and skills can make a huge difference to your bottom line. Graduates contribute approximately £1 billion of added value to the UK economy on an annual basis, according to research by the Association of Graduate Recruiters (AGR).

Ready to mould
You have the opportunity to shape them into what you need, so they become part of the culture. Graduates have developed a habit for learning, so will seek to continuously learn in the working environment. They are often perceived as a 'blank canvas', open to new ideas, ways of working and experiences.

Solid business skills
Studying helps students to develop core transferable skills, such as written and oral communication, problem solving, presentation, organisation and data analysis. Technical graduates will also have up-to-date specialist or technical skills gained from their studies. Many will have experience of applying academic knowledge through work placements, maybe while at a competitor firm.

New perspectives
Graduates can inject new ideas and apply current thinking from academia. Recruiting graduates can also increase diversity within the work team.

Speed to value
Graduates learn more quickly and provide more immediate financial returns. They are more enthusiastic and willing to take on challenges. Graduates understand and have the ability to adapt to change.

Succession planning
Providing career paths for graduates and enabling them to reach management level within your firm will solve succession planning concerns.

What jobs are on offer?

What types of job vacancies are available to graduates when they graduate?

Figure 1 illustrates the main functions to which employers in 2010 were hoping to recruit graduates. As you can see, the most common requirement is to work in finance and IT jobs (these can be jobs in any type of organisation). Based on research carried out by High Fliers, more than half of leading graduate employers were offering jobs in these areas – irrespective of the employers' type of work.

A third of employers anticipated recruiting graduates to work in resources, while up to two-fifths were offering vacancies in engineering. General management remained highly popular – almost half of employers were looking to recruit graduate trainee managers. At the same time, fewer than a fifth of employers were wanting to employ graduates in consulting and investment banking, and just 7% were recruiting graduates for media positions.

These data reveal an important but often misunderstood fact about the graduate job market: there is a large gap between what people think big organisations do and the types of vacancies that they hope to fill. To put it another way: IT companies rarely offer many vacancies. As a result, students often conclude that there are few jobs in IT. But, as Figure 1 shows, the opposite is true. What's different is that it's not just IT firms that want to recruit graduates with IT skills; it's companies across the industrial spectrum – in both the public and the private sectors. The same goes for other specialist subjects and careers. So when it comes to thinking about where to apply, don't judge an employer's recruitment brochure by its cover.

Figure 1: Types of graduate vacancies offered by leading UK employers in 2010
Source: The Graduate Market in 2010, High Fliers Research

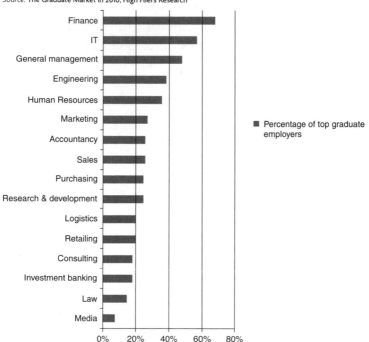

What do employers look for from graduates?

When recruiting graduates, employers look for a range of skills, aptitudes, knowledge and experience. Some of these can be evidenced by your academic background; some of them are more personal, related to who you are and how you might fit in to an organisation. Although your academic background is important for many jobs, qualifications alone are no longer enough to guarantee a graduate job: in today's competitive market for jobs, 'employability skills' are held at a premium.

In fact, when advertising their vacancies, roughly seven out of 10 graduate recruiters ask for 'any' degree subject. Students often find this confusing. How can your degree subject – for three or four years the focal point of your studies – be so easily overlooked by employers?

> " According to a survey of 500 directors, when recruiting, 64% said graduates' employability skills were more important to their firm than the specific occupational, technical or academic skills associated to a degree. "
>
> Institute of Directors, 2007

The answer is this: degree subjects are important to employers, but have to be taken in a wider context of personal skills, attitudes and aptitudes for the job. It's also fair to say that the value of a specific degree subject depends, to a certain extent, on the job itself. Fortunately, no matter how good their personal skills, dentists still need degrees in dentistry; so too do civil engineers, architects, physiotherapists and nurses. However, you'll be surprised at how many employers are happy to recruit graduates with 'any' subject. Accountants, lawyers, bankers, primary school teachers, civil servants, NHS managers, army officers, stock brokers, HR managers, advertising agents and management consultants – none specify which degree you should have studied.

Here, it's probably best to let employers speak for themselves. The following are two recent accounts from leading graduate recruiters in which they define what they are looking for when recruiting graduates.

The first is from Sonja Stockton, head of recruitment at Pricewater houseCoopers. Asked what her firm looks for in graduates, she said:

> " Strong academic performance is a prerequisite ... but those with the employability edge will demonstrate experience and skills gained inside and outside of study. "

Stockton's account is interesting, for it illustrates how leading employers almost take academic achievement for granted; in today's job market, good A levels and a strong degree are no longer selling points – employers expect them. But what does the term 'employability edge' mean? Employers increasingly talk about 'employability skills', but few define what they actually mean by the term. Fortunately, Stephen Green, chief executive of HSBC, has been more forthcoming.

In a newspaper interview in January 2009, Green discussed the range of employability skills that his firm looked for when recruiting graduates. Below is his two-stage answer. First, he sets the scene by illustrating how many applications HSBC receives from graduates each year for its management training schemes.

> We recruit up to 1,500 graduates on to one of our 70 graduate programmes around the world. For those jobs, globally, we receive around 100,000 applications. As 90% have a 2.2 or a 2.1 and will therefore meet our criteria, it takes something extra to stand out.

Next, Green gives an example of what that 'something extra' might be:

> Recent recruits include a graduate who taught English and Spanish in Guatemala; one who ran a restaurant; another who worked in the Beijing Paralympics; a Punjabi singer who's been on TV. Another graduate from Cameroon had published a book and set up a small business selling second hand clothes from New York to Africa, before joining HSBC.

Get the picture? *Welcome to the new world of work!*

Which way to the graduate job market?

The term 'graduate job market' is misleading. In practice, there are a number of graduate job markets, all operating alongside each other. Based on the types of jobs identified previously by Elias and Purcell Table 4 provides an insight into the different job markets that graduates currently face.

Of these five graduate job markets, the most prominent by far is that for modern graduate occupations. These are the jobs and employers that dominate most universities' careers and recruitment events; the organisations with the largest recruitment budgets, the best advertising agencies and the most creative, eye-catching campaigns. Many of these organisations are represented by the Association of Graduate Recruiters (AGR). AGR is very successful at promoting its member organisations, particularly in the media. As a result, AGR organisations can often become the 'voice' of the graduate recruitment market – when in fact such firms represent only one part of the overall opportunities available each year to graduates.

The prominence of AGR organisations means that applications to them are extremely high. This can easily create a distorting effect. The most visible jobs and employers on campus are those which face the largest number of applications and in which chances of success are, by a sheer process of mathematics, the slimmest.

Table 4: An overview of different graduate recruitment markets

	CHARACTERISTICS	TARGET GROUP	WHERE ADVERTISED	PROMINENCE
Traditional	Highly specialist, controlled by professions, eg medicine, architecture, law.	Discrete groups with specialist qualifications. Highly restricted access to vacancies.	Vacancies notified via specialist professional networks, publications and competitions.	Nationally – low. Within professions – very high.
Modern	Blue-chip companies with high levels of brand recognition, often represented by AGR.	All students – particularly those at Russell Group universities.	Careers fairs and campus recruitment events; national job sites; careers directories; national newspapers.	Very high – despite offering fewer than 20,000 vacancies per year.
New	Growing in prominence, usually advertised via university careers sites.	All students – but often targeted at those within geographical regions.	Regionally, via careers service networks and national vacancy sites, eg Graduate Prospects.	Rising – more graduates are seeking to remain in their local region.
Niche	Specialist and ad hoc recruitment patterns; often characterised by small and medium-sized companies.	Primarily targeted at local students. Rarely advertised on a national scale.	Word of mouth and networking. Reliant on direct contact with management.	As yet, low, but likely to rise as more graduates seek niche opportunities.
Non-graduate	Low-pay, low-status jobs.	All – regardless of subject of study, institution, etc.	Job Centres, local newspapers, recruitment agencies.	Low on-campus visibility. May be advertised as part-time jobs.

The top 10 skills on every recruiter's shopping list

According to a survey by AGR, the main reason why graduate recruiters don't fill vacancies is a shortage in the supply of applicants with the right mix of employability skills. Carl Gilleard, chief executive of AGR said:

> Employers are likely to be looking for graduates who can demonstrate softer skills such as team working, cultural awareness, leadership and communication skills, as well as academic achievement.

You'll find these skills cited in many employers' lists. But how do we know that this is what employers really look for when recruiting?

To find out what employers really look for when they are hiring graduates, a major study was undertaken by the University of Sheffield. Its aim was to identify the most in-demand 'skills' required by the majority of recruiters. After analysing over 10,000 job advertisements, researchers had their list:

1. Oral communication
2. Team work
3. Enthusiasm
4. Motivation
5. Initiative
6. Leadership
7. Commitment
8. Interpersonal skills
9. Organisation
10. Foreign language skills

Look again at this list. If you piece these skills together, an image emerges of the ideal graduate that employers look to hire. For a start, he or she has to be good with people — confident, bright, enthusiastic and able to express themselves in different contexts. He or she will be reliable and dependable, capable of working both on alone and in a team. Most of all, this graduate will be organised and highly motivated, a self-starter, someone who gets things done without having to be told. They will also be ready, should the situation arise, to lead a team. In other words, employers want graduates to think and behave like future managers. And all from their first day at work!

Two points from the Sheffield research are worth noting. First, apart from foreign language skills, nothing on the list of ideal graduate skills suggests or denotes a particular degree subject. This 'ideal' graduate could be from any academic background and studying any degree subject – vocational or non-vocational.

The second point is that, when you stop to consider it, 'enthusiasm', 'commitment' and 'motivation' aren't actually 'skills' at all – they're *attitudes*, ways of looking at and approaching the world.

Chapter 3

Old school ties: the importance of where you study

Employers are so convinced they are in a war with each other for a limited supply of talented graduates that they concentrate their marketing on a relatively small number of universities in which they believe that talent is to be found. But don't worry if you didn't go to one of these universities: once you have grasped the formula of employability recruiters won't be able to resist you!

The UK's six categories of university

It is often claimed in the media that where you study for your degree is as important as what you study. But is this true? How important are a university's name and reputation in helping its graduates to find employment? In this chapter, we look at the different types of universities in the UK and the influence that where you study has on your career opportunities. We begin by looking at how higher education is currently structured.

Despite sharing the name 'university', every university in the UK has its own history, character, traditions and way of doing things. But while all universities are different, between some universities there exist certain similarities. For the sake of your future career, it's important to know what they are.

Because universities are so diverse, different groups have emerged to represent the interests of different types of institutions. These include the various regional university associations and the so-called 'mission groups'. The mission groups include the following:

- **The 1994 Group:** so called because of the year when it was founded, consists of 19 UK universities that share common aims, standards and values.

- **The Russell Group:** an association of 20 major research-intensive universities in the United Kingdom. The group is so called because it traditionally met at the Russell Hotel, London.

- **The University Alliance:** formally launched in 2007. Its member institutions have a balanced portfolio of research, teaching, enterprise and innovation as integral to their missions.

However, a large number of universities do not belong to any of these mission groups, but do belong to Universities UK.

In shorthand terms, the UK's universities can be classified into six categories (Table 5).

Table 5: The six categories of UK universities

CATEGORY	ORIGIN
Ancient universities	The seven universities founded between the 12th and 16th centuries
The University of London, the University of Wales and Durham University	Each chartered in the 19th century
Red Brick universities	The six large civic universities chartered at the turn of the 20th century, before the before First World War
Plate Glass universities	The universities chartered in the 1960s (formerly described as the 'new universities')
The Open University	Britain's 'open to all' distance learning university (established in 1968)
New Universities	The post-1992 universities formed from polytechnics or colleges of higher education

The Russell Group

The Russell Group is a collaboration of 20 UK universities that together receive a high proportion of the country's research grants and contract funding. Established in 1994, the group represents the interests of research-intensive universities.

The Russell Group contains many of the United Kingdom's leading universities and 18 of its 20 members are in the top 20 in terms of research funding. When the Russell Group was set up, 19 smaller research universities formed the 1994 Group in response.

As of November 2009, the following universities were members of the Russell Group: Birmingham, Bristol, Cambridge, Cardiff, Edinburgh, Glasgow, Imperial, King's College London, Leeds, Liverpool, London School of

Economics, Manchester, Newcastle, Nottingham, Queens University Belfast, Oxford, Sheffield, Southampton, University College London, Warwick.

Universities and future earnings

Research by Chevalier and Conlon at the London School of Economics has found that studying at a Russell Group university confers a wage premium of approximately 10% compared to modern universities, after accounting for A level scores, parental background, school attended and other factors affecting wages. It is likely that the education provided by Russell Group universities, with its emphasis on the various studies which have been published suggesting that, compared to those from newer universities, graduates from 'older' (ie pre-1992) institutions have an advantage when competing for certain 'graduate' jobs. One of the reasons put forward for this is that graduate recruiters – particularly those from large and prestigious organisations – have a tendency to target their recruitment activities at pre-selected institutions.

This doesn't mean that graduates from non-targeted universities are necessarily disadvantaged; but it does mean that the playing field isn't quite as level as you might have expected it to be. (For more on this, see the final section of this chapter 'The war for talent').

What's in a name?

In early 2009, 10 of the UK's leading graduate recruiters announced that they were to make 60 visits to university campuses. The aim of these visits was simple: to promote the recruiters' organisations and to advertise their graduate vacancies. What's interesting, however, is the universities they chose.

Of these 60 visits, 45 were to universities that were members of the Russell Group – as we already know, an elite group of 20 research-intensive institutions. A further six visits were to members of the 1994 Group. Just four visits were made to new, post-1992 universities.

Of course, just because a firm chooses to attend a university's careers fair doesn't mean that students from other universities are precluded from attending that event, or that they won't be able to apply for the company's jobs. But it does give students at targeted universities an advantage. After all, it means that employers are coming to you, in preference to others. How you use that advantage is up to you.

> **Some Russell Group universities were more than 10 times more likely to be visited by leading recruiters than even the most popular post-1992 universities.**

On a wider level, the issue of employers' targeting activity is controversial, which is one reason why it is rarely acknowledged by employers. This is partly because the expansion of higher education has been based on the principle of fair access to all, and partly because employers are keen to demonstrate their commitment to diversity and equal opportunities.

In practice, however, a different picture often emerges. In recent years, various studies have been published which have sought to explain how and why targeting occurs. The following extract is taken from a book by academics Anthony Hesketh and Philip Brown (2006). They write:

> **Employers are so convinced they are in a war with each other for a limited supply of talented graduates that, despite lots of talk about attracting a diverse range of candidates, they concentrate their marketing on a relatively small number of universities in which they believe that talent is to be found. Students and graduates of those universities are able to use the insights provided by the marketing to gain an advantage over their peers at less prestigious universities,**

particularly in terms of understanding how to present themselves. **"**

Another similar study has found that while Oxford and Cambridge students have a 1 in 8 chance of securing a job with a leading graduate recruiter, those from 'new' universities faced odds of up to 1 in 235.

A study in 2010 by High Fliers identified the top 20 universities likely to be targeted by the largest number of leading graduate recruiters. They are listed in Table 6.

Table 6: Universities targeted by the largest number of top employers in 2010
Source: High Fliers

1. Manchester	11. Durham
2. London	12. Sheffield
3. Warwick	13. Loughborough
4. Cambridge	14. Edinburgh
5. Oxford	15. Southampton
6. Nottingham	16. Newcastle
7. Bath	17. Cardiff
8 Bristol	18. York
9. Leeds	19. Liverpool
10. Birmingham	20. Lancaster

What if you don't study at one of these universities?

For a start, you're unlikely to see as many employers from big-name brands visiting your campus. But this is not all bad news. Most of today's large employers have extensive websites containing lots of information about their graduate recruitment schemes. As long as you meet the basic entry criteria, just because you don't attend a targeted university doesn't mean that you will be unable to get a job with one of these firms.

❝❝ Oxford and Cambridge students have a 1 in 8 chance of securing a job with a leading graduate recruiter. Those from 'new' universities face odds of up to 1 in 235. "

Using the Graduate Prospects website (www.prospects.ac.uk), you can also find out about how you can attend various careers fairs and events that are being hosted by universities in your region. Some of these will be open to students from other universities.

One other point to make is ... so what? Even though visually, large graduate recruiters tend to dominate the recruitment scene, don't forget that most organisations in the UK are small and medium-sized and rarely recruit via traditional graduate recruitment schemes. Instead, they expect you to apply directly to them or via specific vacancies advertised by your careers service. So don't despair. Even though you might not be at a university which finds itself targeted by big employers, your career opportunities are just as bright – but you might have to go out of your way to find opportunities.

The People's Republic of Students

So why do employers target some universities and not others?

Partly, the answer lies in the sheer number of universities in existence. In the past decade, the number of students attending universities in the UK has grown substantially. To give you an idea of just how substantially, consider the following.

Some 2.4 million students are currently enrolled in UK higher education – roughly twice the number of people employed by Britain's largest employer, the NHS. To put it another way, Britain has 20 times more students than it has soldiers in its armed forces.

But compared to other countries, such figures are far from exceptional. Since the late 1980s, student numbers have been growing on a global scale. Today, being a student is the world's second most popular occupation – the most popular, reputedly, being a soldier in the Chinese People's Army. Unfortunately, not all employers enjoy the same limitless capacity to grow. In fact, for many, the challenge is how to reduce headcount, not increase it.

In 2009, nearly 400,000 students graduated from UK universities. Of these, most were headed for the job market. Rising student numbers have posed a serious problem for the way in which graduate recruiters operate. Employers in high-profile organisations have found themselves deluged with applications and CVs – many of which they receive on-line.

All of this, you might think, would be fantastic news for recruiters. After all, all they have to do is advertise their vacancies and then wait for the applications to roll in. In fact, the opposite is true, because graduate recruiters are locked into a costly and escalating war – a war seemingly without aims, a war which some claim can never be won. Unlike real wars, however, this one was caused by the publication of a report.

The war for talent

The idea of a 'war for talent' (as mentioned earlier on page 3) is an often-cited explanation for why many leading employers target some universities more than others. But what does it mean?

The term 'war for talent' first appeared in a report by the consultancy firm McKinsey in the late 1990s. Since then, it has influenced many firms' recruitment strategies. Underpinning the 'war for talent' are four inter-linked concepts:

> Some 2.4 million students are currently enrolled in UK higher education – roughly twice the number of people employed by Britain's largest employer, the NHS. To put it another way, Britain has 20 times more students than it has soldiers in its armed forces.

- To be successful in future markets, organisations will be increasingly dependent on employee 'talent'.

- This 'talent' is in short supply – despite the huge increase in the number of people around the world going to university.

- As companies become increasingly the same, the only way they will be able to compete with each other is through 'talent'. This gives enormous advantages to 'talented' employees.

- In order to recruit, retain and motivate 'talented' employees, organisations need highly tuned recruitment strategies that help them to target the best candidates as speedily and efficiently as possible. Failure to do so could be disastrous.

To demonstrate just how much the world of work has changed, the report's authors drew up the chart in Table 7 to show the extent to which the 'Old Reality' of work and attitudes to employees had been superseded by the 'New Reality' (Table 7). The message from McKinsey was clear. The future was bright, but only if that future was based on 'talent.'

Table 7: The changing reality of work
Source: E. Michaels, H. Handfield-Jones and B. Axelrod (1997).

THE OLD REALITY	THE NEW REALITY
People need companies	Companies need people
Machines capital and geography are the competitive advantage	Talented people are the competitive advantage
Better talent makes some difference	Better talent makes a huge difference
Jobs are scarce	Talented people are scarce
Employees are loyal and people are secure	People are mobile and their commitment is short term
People accept the standard package they are offered	People demand much more

Chapter 4

Graduate destinations

For many, the first few months after university are a time when they are most reliant on their degree; later in a graduate's career other factors become more important – work experience, contacts, on-the-job training and specialist knowledge.

The graduate destinations survey

When Elvis Presley died in 1977 there were 37 Elvis impersonators in the world. By 1993 there were 48,000. At that rate, by 2010, one in three people in the world will be employed as an Elvis impersonator.

Uh-huh. Relying on statistics, particularly when making career predictions, is always a risky business. As the above piece of mathematical gymnastics proves, a prediction that makes sense to a statistician doesn't always work out that way in real life. Just because something glistens doesn't mean to say that it's a gold lamé jumpsuit.

However, because it's likely that the degree you study will have a significant bearing on your future career, it's important that before you sign up for any course you know what graduates from that subject go on to do after university. After all, no one these days buys a holiday without scanning internet sites such as TripAdvisor to see how previous customers have rated the hotel or resort. The same principle applies to university courses. If you want to know what sort of jobs you can do with a certain subject, what better way than finding out what graduates from past years have gone on to do?

Three things you need to know about statistics

Statistics never exist in a vacuum. How can they? Think where they've been, where they came from, the number of times they've swapped hands. In fact,

> **There are three kinds of lies: lies, damned lies, and statistics.**
>
> Mark Twain

no matter how hard you scrub them statistics are always *infected* — they always come to you with traces of other people's opinions, attitudes and agendas.

Second, statistics *never* speak for themselves. Instead, they need an interpreter, a translator, and an on-hand critic – someone who asks, 'Yes, but how do I know this is true?' In the absence of these three experts, you need to train yourself to do all three jobs, to keep all three voices in your head.

Third, to bring them alive, statistics need stories – powerful narratives and convincing storylines in which statistics make sense. Without a storyline, statistics are ... well, simply random numbers. With a story, statistics can help you to plan the greatest story of them all: your future. But remember: it has to be *your* story, not someone else's.

This chapter will show you what graduates in different subjects have gone on to after university – the jobs that they have entered, the sorts of organisations that they have gone to work for, even how much they have earned. This information is essential, for it will give you a direct insight into the value of degree courses in today's workplace.

But before you look at the tables, please take time to read the first part of this chapter, which will give you a short overview of the graduate job market, particularly in terms of how it has changed since the credit crunch. Only by understanding how this market is changing can you fully appreciate the value of the statistical stories that follow.

Trends and predictions

Each year, university careers services carry out a nationwide survey into what students do after leaving higher education. Data from this survey offers a fascinating glimpse into the changing world of graduate careers.

Like all large-scale research, the survey has its limitations. For a start, because it takes place within several months of students' graduation, data generated from it reveals only those jobs and courses that students have secured in the first six months after graduating. For most people, these months are a time of considerable change and upheaval. Because of this, first jobs are rarely long-term jobs.

But at the same time, several factors are undoubtedly in the survey's favour. What students do after university *matters* – to them, to their families, to their universities – and in particular, to *you*. First jobs might not be long-term jobs, but they are important jobs; jobs that can all too often set the pattern for a long-term career.

Capturing first destinations can also be helpful in revealing how buoyant the job market is for new graduates. For many, the first few months after university are a time when they are most reliant on their degree; later in a graduate's career other factors become more important – work experience, contacts, on-the-job training and specialist knowledge.

The information in this chapter is the most up to date available and was collected by university careers services from UK and European Union graduates who completed their undergraduate courses at British universities in 2008. The survey is comprehensive – just under a quarter of a million graduates (220,065) took part.

To give you a long-term view of what graduates do, Table 8 compares the overall first destinations of UK graduates between the years 2006 and 2008. From this, several key points stand out, which are reviewed in the remaining sections of this chapter.

Table 8: Three-year comparison of graduate destinations
Source: AGCAS

	Number responding to the destination survey	(a) Entering employment	(b) Entering further study/training	(c) Working and studying	(d) Unemployed at time of survey	(e) Other
2008	220,065	61.4%	14.1%	8.1.%	7.9%	8.5%
2007	209,120	63.3%	13.9%	9.1%	5.5%	8.3%
2006	209,245	62.9%	13.8%	9.0%	6.0%	8.3%

Included with the permission of AGCAS and HESCU. For the latest version of this publication see www.prospects.ac.uk. For permission to reproduce, contact copyright@ agcas.org.uk and copyright@prospects.ac.uk.

The 'crunch' factor

The first point to emerge from the survey is that there was clearly a 'crunch' factor which impacted on graduate careers in 2008 – although not as extensively as might have been expected. Compared to 2007, the class of 2008 were slightly less likely to be employed, and more likely to be unemployed. The overall drop in employment is probably not very significant – if 2006 is taken into consideration, it probably suggests that 2007 was a very strong year for employment.

The unemployment column of the table is more revealing. Since the early 1990s graduate unemployment has been low, and despite a slight rise in 2006, the 5.5% recorded for 2007 was in line with overall trends over several years. A jump of almost four percentage points in a year reveals that the market for graduates was obviously beginning to contract by 2008, and that fewer opportunities for graduates were available.

Even so, conditions for the class of 2008 appear to have been relatively buoyant. If you add together columns a, b and c it becomes clear that within six months of leaving university, more than eight out of 10 (83.6%) graduates, were either in work, in further study or enrolled on a professional training course.

Figure 2 provides a somewhat different picture of the graduate job market – certainly, different from that presented over the past year by certain elements of the national press. It suggests that while a crunch factor can definitely be traced in the destinations of 2008 graduates, actual market conditions were not as bad as some journalists had predicted.

Figure 2: An overview of UK graduate destinations
Source: AGCAS

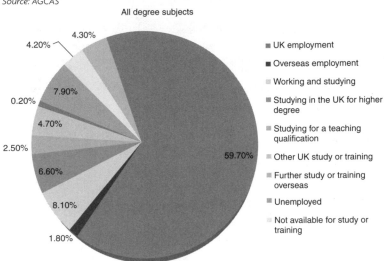

Included with the permission of AGCAS and HESCU. For the latest version of this publication see www.prospects.ac.uk. For permission to reproduce, contact copyright@agcas.org.uk and copyright@prospects.ac.uk.

Calculating the benefits of postgraduate study

One point to emerge clearly from the data is that the higher your educational qualifications are, the less chance you have of being unemployed.

Postgraduate students – those with higher degrees such as Master's and doctorates – are considerably less likely to face unemployment than those with first degrees, eg bachelor-level qualifications (Table 9). This is partly to be expected, perhaps. Postgraduate study offers a range of advantages: specialist skills and knowledge, higher-level learning, even the chance to work on projects that are closely related to industry. But a postgraduate degree by itself is no insurance against the threat of unemployment. Employers often argue that while they are keen to recruit those with higher qualifications, postgraduates have to demonstrate their worth (and perhaps slightly more than undergraduates). And remember: a postgraduate degree is no automatic guarantee of higher earnings.

Table 9: What graduates from different modes of study do

	WORK ONLY	WORK AND STUDY	STUDY ONLY	UNEMPLOYED	TOTAL RETURNS
Full-time postgraduate	78.1%	7.4%	7.1%	4.2%	38,620
Full-time first degree	63.0%	7.6%	15.5%	8.5%	191,740
Part-time postgraduate	79.1%	12.5%	2.8%	1.8%	26,780
Part-time first degree	66.6%	15.1%	5.9%	5.2%	21,530

How many graduates get 'graduate' jobs?

Using Elias and Purcell's job categories, it is possible to work out how many graduates from 2007 entered traditional, modern, new, niche and non-graduate jobs. Table 10 illustrates the proportions of graduates entering these categories of jobs. From this, you can see how 'graduate' occupations account for 66.5% of all jobs undertaken by graduates in the first six months after graduation. Of these, just 11.7% were 'traditional' graduate jobs; whereas 'niche' occupations – nurses, retail managers, graphic designers, etc – accounted for over one third of all destinations. Worryingly,

> Six months after graduation, exactly one third of the class of 2007 were in jobs for which a degree qualification was not required – further proof that in today's graduate job market, just having a degree doesn't necessarily mean that you are destined for graduate-level occupations.

33.5% of graduates entered 'non-graduate' jobs – jobs for which degree-level qualifications were not required. No one can be sure how many of these graduates were still in such jobs a year later; and no one knows if these were 'stop-gap' jobs. What we do know, however, is that for today's graduates, under-employment (working in a job for which you are over-qualified) is a bigger risk than unemployment.

Table 10: Proportion of graduates employed in different types of jobs
Source: AGCAS

TYPES OF JOB	EXAMPLES	2007
Traditional graduate occupations	Medical practitioners, dentists, architects, lawyers	11.7%
Modern graduate occupations	Software programmers, journalists, primary school teachers, graduate management trainees	13.8%
New graduate occupations	Marketing, management accountants, therapists and many forms of engineer	17.2%
Niche graduate occupations	Nursing, retail managers, graphic designers	23.8%
Non-graduate occupations	Any jobs that do not fall into the above categories.	33.5%
All		100%
Total in graduate occupations		66.5%

Included with the permission of AGCAS and HESCU. For the latest version of this publication see www.prospects.ac.uk. For permission to reproduce, contact copyright@agcas.org.uk and copyright@prospects.ac.uk.

Where in the UK are graduate jobs located?

Plotting where graduates go to work after leaving university can reveal interesting information both on the state of the economy and on the distribution of jobs. Using data compiled by HESA, it is possible to look at where a sample of graduates from 2008 – those who went directly into employment – were based within six months of graduation.

Table 14 provides the answer. The overwhelming majority of 2008 graduates secured employment in England (82.4%), with Scotland, Wales and Northern Ireland combined accounting for just 16.9% of the total UK graduate employment market.

But take a closer look at where the 82.4% of graduates employed in England were working. More than one in four (27.8%) were based in London and the South East – by far the biggest concentration of graduates in the UK, and further proof of how this region continues to be the economic engine room of the UK.

Table 11: Geographical distribution of UK 2007–8 graduates
Source: HESA

TOTAL FIRST DEGREE	148,485	PERCENTAGE
Total England	122,490	82.4
North East	5,365	3.6
North West	16,435	11
Yorkshire and The Humber	10,540	7.0
East Midlands	9,500	6.3
West Midlands	12,590	8.4
East of England	13,120	8.8
London	19,695	13.2
South East	21,740	14.6
South West	12,745	8.5
Wales	7,240	4.8
Scotland	12,170	8.1
Northern Ireland	5,945	4.0
Guernsey, Jersey and the Isle of Man	505	0.3

Figure 3: Location of graduate vacancies at leading UK employers
Source: High Fliers, 2010

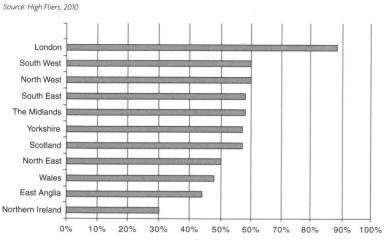

But why are so many graduates concentrated in London and the South East? It may be partly because that's where many of the jobs are located.

Research by High Fliers has found that, in 2010, almost 90% of leading large organisations were offering graduate vacancies in London. More than half of these also planned to recruit graduates for jobs in the South East of England (Figure 4). But if you don't live in London and the South East, don't panic. High Fliers' research uncovered another five regions where more than 50% of recruiters were targeting their vacancies. These included the South West, North West, Midlands, Yorkshire and Scotland. The North East and Wales were not far behind.

If you live in a region targeted by relatively fewer graduate recruiters, don't despair. All it means is that you are going to have to work harder to catch employers' attention. Following the employability formula will help; so too will making sure that you use every possible opportunity to develop your employability skills.

Who are the most employable – men or women?

At universities, women now outnumber men – an incredible turnaround, given that until the First World War women were banned by the universities from graduating with degrees. Since then, the tables have been turned for good.

Women are also more successful in the job market – at least in the early years after graduation. Not only do a higher proportion of women every year enter employment, but women are also more likely to engage in jobs which enable them to keep studying. Women's unemployment is also markedly lower than that of men (Table 11).

Table 12: Differences between male and female graduates' early career experiences

FULL TIME FIRST DEGREE	WORK ONLY	WORK AND STUDY	STUDY ONLY	UNEMPLOYED	TOTAL RETURNS
Female	64.8%	8.0%	15.2%	6.8%	110,940
Male	60.6%	7.1%	15.9%	10.8%	80,795

Recession and the lure of the public sector

For graduates, recession has a habit of making careers in the public sector suddenly look more appealing. In the past two years, 'recession-goggles' have done wonders for careers in teaching, the armed forces, NHS and public utilities. In 2009, applications for the NHS management programme shot up by 83%. Applications to teacher training also rose, by almost 14%.

Do these students really want to teach — or is it a case of any classroom in a storm? A survey of 16,000 students by High Fliers found teaching was the most popular career choice of 2009. In 2008, students ranked it third. Unsurprisingly, investment banking fell from second to ninth position.

Enter the dragon's den: becoming your own boss

Organisationally based careers are not your only option. Every year, around 5,000 graduates complete their university studies before setting up their own businesses. Perhaps they are spurred on by TV programmes such as *Dragon's Den*, because a career as an entrepreneur is becoming increasingly popular — and the government is keen to encourage more students to start their own businesses.

E = Employability

Currently, 3.7% of degree holders start their own businesses in the first six months after university. This might not sound much, but percentages need to be viewed in a historical context, otherwise they can be misleading. Over the past decade the percentage has almost doubled, and analysts claim that it is set to rise further.

But when it comes to self-employment, some degree subjects are more likely than others to produce budding Richard Bransons. Traditionally, dentists, vets and various types of medical practitioners have had high levels of self-employment and have tended to dominate surveys on self-employment.

Table 12 shows other degree subjects offering the highest percentages of graduates going into self-employment. As before, the percentages are a snapshot taken within six months of graduation. The actual long-term figures for self-employment is likely to be substantially greater.

Table 13: **Degree subjects with the highest numbers of self-employed graduates, 2007–8**
Source: HESA

SUBJECT	PERCENTAGE
Design studies	14.3%
Drama	7.8%
Music	7.3%
Fine Art	5.4%
Cinematics and photography	3.9%
Computer science	3.5%
Business Studies	3.3%
Complementary medicine	3.1%
Media studies	3.1%
Sports science	2.9%
English studies	2.5%
Psychology	2.2%
Other subjects	40.8%

Note: Subjects such as dentistry, medicine and veterinary science are not included in this table.

From this you can see that artistic and creative subjects top the list – with over 14% of design studies graduates starting their own businesses. Mostly, they were self-employed designers, engaged in a wide variety of fashion, product and media-related design work.

But it's not just academic discipline that affects your chances of becoming self-employed; geographical location is also a contributing factor. Just under 28% of graduates who reported themselves as self-employed were based in London. A further 12% were located in the South East. The North West was home to 8.5% of graduate entrepreneurs, while a further 8.1% worked in the South West. Graduates from the North East were the least likely to set up their own businesses, with 2.4% entering self-employment.

In the past decade, the profile of self-employment has increased across higher education, and universities are now far more active in terms of encouraging and supporting their students in developing entrepreneurial career ideas. At the same time, far greater support is available for students and graduates via Business Link and Regional Development Agencies (see the section on further reading at the end of this book).

The question you will need to consider, if self-employment appeals to you, is at what stage to embark on your business idea. As we have seen, for some disciplines, eg art and design, self-employment is an established career pattern. For others it is still relatively rare, and many students opt to spend several years working for an organisa-tion, gaining experience, making contacts, paying off debts and gaining added commercial awareness. Only after that do they make the move into self-employment.

Whichever route you take, you will need to ensure that, before starting your own business, you take time (and specialist advice) so as to develop a watertight business plan.

Case study: Dimitar

Dimitar is a Bulgarian student who has recently completed a Master's degree in Business Management. While studying in the UK he became aware of the growing possibilities for organising travel tours to rural parts of Bulgaria. Using his contacts and local expertise – including his first-hand insight into the cultural differences between the UK and Bulgaria – he drew up a business plan and entered a competition for young entrepreneurs. His business idea was relatively simple. Using his contacts within the Bulgarian travel industry he would market and promote special educational tours for UK students and school parties. These would be promoted via a website developed by Dimitar in partnership with two computer science students.

As part of the young entrepreneur competition, Dimitar was offered a mentor – a local business person with special expertise in internet-based business. Together, they reworked the business plan, smoothing it out and offering prospective customers far greater value for money. When the time came to 'pitch' to the competition judges, Dimitar was fairly confident that his business plan was nearly unbeatable. His confidence shone through and he won first prize – a cheque for £5,000.

Since the competition, Dimitar has graduated and has started taking his first groups of tourists to the mountain region of Bulgaria. Although his business has been adversely affected by the credit crunch, he is confident that when the market picks up he will be in a good position to capitalise.

Dimitar puts his entrepreneurial spirit down to his family background and his academic training, which has given him a powerful insight into how businesses operate. He also thinks being self-employed is a lifestyle choice; while it suits him, he is the first to admit that it's not for everyone.

Chapter 5

Show me the money!

Many people find it difficult to talk about money – particularly at job interviews. It's hardly surprising, then, that so many graduates should be so poorly prepared when negotiating starting salaries with their prospective employers.

All about 'average' salaries

What graduates earn is almost as hot a topic as what graduates do after leaving university. The economic downturn has served to intensify the discussion. After all, going to university represents a sizeable investment. The question is: will this investment pay off?

Graduate earnings for different subjects and subject clusters are

66 For 2007 graduates working full time in the UK, the average starting salary was £19,300 – a 4.3% increase on the £18,501 recorded in the previous year. 99

explored in further detail in Chapter 6. This chapter provides an overview of graduate earnings across all subjects.

There are several things you need to know about graduate salaries. The first is that there is no commonly agreed 'average'. Instead, there are lots of widely debated 'averages'. Which average you choose to believe is, to some extent, up to you. It also depends on where you live, what type of 'graduate' job you call home, and which source of data you're quoting.

What we do know is that average salaries tend to be higher if you are employed by one of the traditional or modern graduate employers discussed in Chapter 1. Such employers generally pay above 'average' starting salaries. The fact that many of them are located in London and the South East also makes a difference. Generally, the closer you are to London, the higher the earnings.

For 2007 graduates working full time in the UK, the average starting salary was £19,300 – a 4.3% increase on the £18,501 recorded for the previous year. Graduates whose first job was based in London received the highest pay: £22,479. Second-highest earners were those working in the South East.

Table 13 reveals some of the salaries earned by 2007 graduates by type of work. Health service professionals – doctors, dentists and pharmacists

– secured the highest individual earnings. These were followed by professional managers.

Table 14: Top 10 average salaries by type of work
Source: Destinations of Leavers from Higher Education Institutions, 2007-08, HESA

	TYPE OF JOB	AVERAGE SALARY FOR A NEW GRADUATE
1.	Health professionals (eg doctors, dentists and pharmacists)	£24,968
2.	Production managers	£23,573
3.	Professional managers	£22,942
4.	Engineers	£22,823
5.	Business and statistical jobs (eg accountants, management consultants, economists)	£22,535
6.	Information and communications technology (ICT)	£22,244
7.	Architects, town planners, surveyors	£20,472
8.	Teaching (eg secondary and primary school teachers)	£19,577
9.	Legal professions	£19,550
10.	Quality and customer care managers	£19,540
	All types of jobs	£19,300

But within the statistics lurk many fascinating, and at times contentious, stories.

'Average' salary tables imply that two graduates with identical qualifications starting work in the same jobs on the same day start work on the same salary. They don't. Not if the graduates in question are male and female.

The gender pay gap

The 'Great Brain Robbery'

After almost 30 years of legislation, women graduates still earn less than men, and the pay gap widens with age. The question is, why?

Many people find it difficult to talk about money – particularly at job interviews. Perhaps that's because, socially, talking about money is still considered vulgar. It's hardly surprising, then, that so many graduates should be so poorly prepared when negotiating starting salaries with their prospective employers. But what is a surprise is that when it comes to naming a figure, the evidence suggests that women are considerably worse at it than men.

> After 40 years of equality legislation:
>
> - 95% of childcare workers are female
> - 99% of construction workers are male
> - 15% of IT executives are female
> - 99% of plumbers are male
> - 8% of engineers are female
>
> *Source: EOC, 2005*

The on-going pay differential between women and men is hard to explain, particularly given that, on average, women are better qualified and generally more employable than men.

Strange, but true: a 24-year-old female graduate earns on average 15% less than her male counterpart. Seven years on, this pay gap rises to 18%.

Case study: Isobel

Isobel has recently graduated with a degree in History. At the time of writing, she is considering several career options – social work, human resources, and teaching. Her main priority is choose a job that involves working with people: 'I want to do something that I believe in, something that I feel matters.' Any consideration of money is secondary. 'Obviously, I want to earn a reasonable wage, but that's not the be all and end all. I'd much rather do something that I believe in, rather than just earning lots of money.' When asked what she thinks a 'reasonable' wage might be, she laughs. 'I've never really thought about money. In all my part-time jobs, I've always been paid by the hour. I wouldn't have a clue about how much I should be earning as a graduate. No one's ever talked about it.'

Things seem unlikely to change any time soon. Research by the Higher Education Statistical Agency (HESA) into the first-career earnings of 2007 graduates proved that even now, the differential between male and female graduates still applied. For example, in 2007 the median salary for male first-degree graduates working in the UK was £20,000. For females it was £19,000. As in previous years, the highest-paid jobs still went to male graduates – a tradition that seems set to

> 66 **Average annual earnings of female graduates aged 20-24 were £14,592, compared with £16,738 for males.** 99

run and run. The pay gap was even greater among male and female part-time students (here, earnings were £28,000 and £24,000 respectively).

In the past, the pay gap was shrugged off, with vague allusions to differences between women's and men's skills and aspirations. This is no longer possible. Today, as we have already seen, more women than men go to university – an incredible development, bearing in mind that a century ago, barely 1,000 women were enrolled in UK higher education. Not only do women outnumber men in higher education, in academic terms they make better students, recording more first and upper second-class degrees.

Women also have more to gain from university than men. This is another reason why the pay gap is so perplexing. Graduate Prospects (www.prospects.ac.uk) found that, in comparison with men and women with just two A levels, male graduates earned 20% more per hour, while women graduates earned 35% more per hour. The salary premium was even higher for women with Master's degrees (54% more per hour) or doctorates (60% more per hour). So what's going on?

The problem seems to be partly economic, partly social.

Studies have found that not only do women earn less, they *expect* to earn less. Research undertaken among male and female undergraduates suggests that, by the start of their final year, women already have salary expectations that are lower than men's. In other words, even before entering the job market, women expect to earn lower salaries. Once they are in a job, this rapidly becomes a self-fulfilling prophecy. If you expect less, you generally receive less.

The geek shall inherit the earth

Another theory as to why women graduates earn less than men is that the subjects women study lead to lower-paying jobs. Statistics underpinning this claim are interesting. Research shows that graduates in more technically complex subjects consistently out-earn those in art and humanities subjects. Top of the pay league are business and computing,

> " A large income is the best recipe for happiness I ever heard of. "
>
> Jane Austen

followed by mathematics, law and engineering. Although the number of women entering these subjects has increased in recent years, they remain very much in the minority.

Even so, this theory fails to explain why the gender pay gap remains the same even when women have studied the same subjects, achieved the same grades and are working in the same jobs as men. For example, among graduates with first or upper second-class degrees, the difference between male and female salaries ranges from 20% in law, mathematics and computing, to just 3% in education.

If you are a woman, you should consider these findings carefully. Women have made great advances towards full equality in the workplace, but the salary gap requires explanation. One headline recently claimed that between 1974 and 1998 the number of women company directors increased by a 'stunning' 600%. But take a closer look at the statistics. Despite the 600% increase, the actual proportion of women directors still stood at just 3.6%. In other words, fewer than four in every 100 company directors were women – hardly a 'stunning' triumph for equal opportunities.

Figure 4: Percentages of women and men in selected job sectors

Source: Data Supplied by Northwest Regional Development Agency

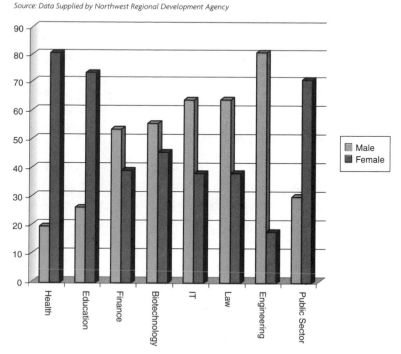

It's time to end the hype. Figure 3 reveals the extent to which employment markets are still dominated by traditional sex-role stereotypes. Despite high-profile role models, most women remain employed in just a handful of job categories. Typically, these are dominated by health, education and the public services. Women are also disproportionately represented in low-paid jobs. Men, on the other hand, dominate all branches of IT, law, biotechnology and engineering.

Till debt do us part?

No female student can afford to be complacent about the gender pay gap, because financially, higher education costs women marginally more than it does men. One study has found that it takes women an extra four years to pay off their student debts. According to data compiled by the House of Commons Library:

> Half a woman's working life will be spent paying off the cost of her higher education. A woman graduate who goes on to have two children will on average take almost 20 years to pay off her debts.

Because you're worth it

There is absolutely no reason why women should carry on earning less than men – particularly given the disproportionate investment made by women in higher education. But what's needed isn't more legislation. What women need is a completely new way of looking at the 'trade-offs' made when thinking about careers and money. Only then will women graduates achieve real equality.

No one is saying that money is the most important factor when applying for a job; but these days the cost of going to university is so great that few people can afford to be blasé about graduate earnings. Remember also that the figures quoted in these gender surveys are always averages. Within them are many discrepancies and variations. Every year, despite what the press write, many women graduates secure high-paying jobs. Ultimately, how important your earnings are to your career is up to you. As the Americans say, 'Do the math'.

Improve your earning potential

If you want to look at how you might be able to improve your earning potential, consider the following possible 'trade-off' ideas.

- **Trade-off #1:** Trade 'Money's not the most important thing for me,' for 'I want a job which pays a wage commensurate with my qualifications/ experience/skills.'

- **Trade-off #2:** Trade jobs with high levels of personal fulfilment for jobs that pay more money. Turn the laws of supply and demand to your advantage. Seek jobs for which you need hard-to-get skills, or for which you have to get further qualifications. Better still, choose jobs that are seen by others as 'nerdy' (eg tax accountant versus PR consultant); or even better, jobs that involve relocation, travel or unsociable hours.

- **Trade-off #3:** Trade job security for job insecurity. Faced with risk, most people sprint for cover. But think again. If you're serious about earning more money, don't automatically rule out jobs that bring with them some degree of financial uncertainty (eg sales commission versus steady income).

- **Trade-off #4:** Trade financial ignorance for financial expertise. When applying for a job you must be fully aware of the going rate for that industry – not just that organisation. Become an expert on how much people in that field not only do earn, but also *can* earn.

- **Trade-off #5:** Trade 'people' jobs for 'techno' jobs. Those who commit to acquiring hard-to-learn skills often reap the benefits in the job market. Saving the planet can be done in evenings and weekends, once the business of making money has been accomplished.

E =
Employability,
Q =
Qualifications,
WE = Work
Experience,
S = Strategies
and
C = Contacts

$$E = Q + WE + S \times C$$

"Do not worry about your difficulties in Mathematics. I can assure you mine are still greater."

Albert Einstein

Chapter 6

The importance of choosing the right subject

The most important consideration is educational – to make sure that you choose a subject that you are going to enjoy studying for the next three or four years. Your career is your second consideration.

Put your subject first

Universities offer literally thousands of degree course qualifications, ranging from golf course management to astrophysics. But before you choose which degree qualification is right for you, it's essential that you know what your options are after graduation. The fact is, when it comes to graduate careers, not all degree qualifications can offer you the same career opportunities.

This chapter looks at how the subject you choose at university will shape the early years of your career. But it's not all about careers. When you are choosing a degree subject the most important consideration is educational – to make sure that you choose a subject that you are going to enjoy studying for the next three or four years. After all, unless you enjoy your course you're unlikely to excel at it. The matter of what you choose to study poses a major risk, because unhappy students rarely make successful students – thus jeopardising the first letter in the employability formula: 'Q' (qualifications).

Your career is your second consideration.

As you are about to discover, among different degree subjects differences now exist between the proportion of graduates who are employed, who are enrolled on further study courses and who, at the time of survey, were unemployed. That's not to say that any one degree course can offer you a watertight guarantee of employment; nor is any degree subject actively avoided by employers. As we saw in Section 1, your chances of getting a job are affected by a whole range of factors, including geographical location, which university you study at and what type of employer you apply to.

How subjects compare

Different degree courses produce different levels of employment, further study and unemployment. Table 15, which presents the subjects with the highest (and the lowest) levels of employment, further study and unemployment, provides a brief summary of some of these differences. Data such as these often generate heated debate, particularly among academics. Tutors often complain that these statistics can be misleading because they present only those destinations recorded within the first six months of graduation.

Table 15: Degree subjects with the highest (and lowest) employment, further study and unemployment
Source: AGCAS

	EMPLOYMENT	FURTHER STUDY	UNEMPLOYMENT
Highest	Medicine, dentistry (94.3%)	Law (53.9%)	Computer science (14.6%)
Second highest	Veterinary science (87.3%)	Mathematics (37.8%)	Mass communications (12.1%)
Third highest	Subjects allied to medicine (84.9%)	Physical sciences (34%)	Creative arts, design (11.2%)
Third lowest	History, philosophy (60.2%)	Medicine, dentistry (10.6%)	Subjects allied to medicine
Second lowest	Physical sciences (56.2%)	Mass communications (10.3%)	Education (3.2%)
Lowest	Law (45.5%)	Veterinary science (7.8%)	Medicine, dentistry (0.2%)

Included with the permission of AGCAS and HESCU. For the latest version of this publication see www.prospects.ac.uk. For permission to reproduce, contact copyright@ agcas.org.uk and copyright@prospects.ac.uk.

But this is to ignore two important points. First, the data are very robust and based on large samples of graduates. So they're reliable. Second, exploring what graduates do in the early months after leaving university is a valid exercise – after all, it gives you a direct insight into the nature of the job market for new graduates.

For you and your future career, knowing what graduates from your chosen subject do directly after university is extremely useful. So what *do* the data tell us?

First, subjects that are allied to medicine, dentistry and veterinary science have some of the highest levels of employment in the UK. This is partly to be expected. Routes into these professions are carefully monitored and controlled; seldom are more graduates recruited to these subjects than there are jobs for them on graduation.

The subject with the lowest levels of employment is law. Again, however (as you will see in the section on Business courses below), there is an explanation for this. To become a solicitor or barrister you need to complete professional training at a university or legal centre. Thus, relatively few law graduates leave university on completion of their degree course; instead, they enrol for further study. Proof of this can be found at the top of the middle column of Table 15. Law has the lowest level of employment and the highest level of further study.

Computer science graduates have the highest level of unemployment – a reflection perhaps of the impact of the recession on IT-related jobs.

Degree subjects with the best (and worst) starting salaries

Data compiled by HESA have shown considerable differences between academic subjects in terms of how much money graduates in these subjects go on to earn in the first year after university (Table 16). So great has this gap become that the pay differential between the highest and the lowest paying academic subjects is now over £12,000 a year.

> **For most graduate jobs, achieving a high grade in your degree is essential. Sixty-seven per cent of graduate recruiters insist on a 2:1 or above. Only 26% insist on a particular degree subject.**

Table 16: Top 10 degrees with the highest starting salaries
Source: HESA

SUBJECT	GRADUATE EMPLOYMENT OR SELF-EMPLOYMENT	NON-GRADUATE EMPLOYMENT OR SELF-EMPLOYMENT
Medicine	£28,897	-
Dentistry	£28,813	-
Chemical engineering	£26,366	£16,553
Economics	£25,101	£17,316
Veterinary medicine	£24,762	
General engineering	£23,876	£15,349
Mechanical engineering	£23,572	£17,426
Middle Eastern and African studies	£23,414	£17,692
Civil engineering	£23,387	£15,444
Social work	£23,328	£15,572

It almost goes without saying that all of this must be carefully considered before you decide which subject to study at university.

As Table 16 illustrates, medicine and dentistry are currently generating the highest graduate starting salaries, followed by chemical engineering. In each of these cases a shortage of skilled professionals explains the high starting salaries. It's also noticeable that graduates in medicine and dentistry – unlike those in almost every other subject – rarely begin their careers in non-graduate jobs. Equally, self-employment is hardly ever an option for these graduates.

Chemical engineering is an in-demand subject. Not only are chemical engineers highly sought after by pharmaceutical firms, their skills make them highly marketable on the international stage, hence the high starting salaries. Self-employment is an option that chemical engineers are willing to pursue, but as the data shows, being self-employed – in the first few years at least – means being prepared to take an inevitable pay cut.

Economics is a completely different matter. Because of their attractiveness to the banking and financial services sector, economics graduates remain among the best-paid graduates in the UK – a fact which sets them apart from university business school graduates. Even after the credit crunch, some economics graduates have continued to attract relatively high salaries, although the buoyancy of these salaries is likely to be reduced somewhat in the coming years.

Among the top 10 best-paying subjects, perhaps only Middle Eastern and African studies look out of place. But again there are good reasons behind these subjects' high earnings potential – most of them related to oil and oil exploration. In recent years, demand for new oil fields has led oil firms to drill further afield in Africa and in new areas of the Middle East. Suddenly, graduates with a good understanding of these parts of the world are in demand – and, as a result, their earning potential has increased. Graduates in these subjects are also, for the time being, comparatively rare (another factor guaranteed to boost earnings potential). This cannot be said for some other degree subjects.

Table 17 looks at the degree subjects with the lowest average graduate starting salaries. It is interesting to note that the factors which in Tables 13–20 led to high earnings, ie tightly controlled professional training courses (medicine), skills that are highly sought after by big businesses (chemical engineering), or the fact that graduates in these subjects are sought after by business while at the same time being relatively scarce (Middle Eastern studies), are mostly absent among these subjects, thus resulting in lower starting salaries.

Table 17: Degree subjects with the lowest starting salaries
Source: HESA

SUBJECT	GRADUATE EMPLOYMENT OR SELF-EMPLOYMENT	NON-GRADUATE EMPLOYMENT OR SELF-EMPLOYMENT
Agriculture and forestry	£18,333	£15,047
Sociology	£18,293	£14,528
Psychology	£18,091	£13,999
Linguistics	£17,681	£14,535
Communication and media studies	£17,549	£14,484
Art and design	£17,327	£14,086
Drama, dance and cinematics	£17,260	£14,340
Archaeology	£17,065	£14,473
Music	£17,017	£14,217
Celtic studies	£16,604	£16,524

You can see from this table that graduates in these subjects are also more likely to enter lower-paid non-graduate first jobs.

But if your heart is set on studying dance at university or, for that matter, Celtic studies, it's important that you put these data into context. The figures quoted are averages, and within each category graduates in these subjects will have earned significantly higher (and lower) salaries. The important point is that you are aware of these facts and you take appropriate steps to make sure that at every opportunity you build up your skills, knowledge, work experience and contacts.

Chapter 7

The qualifications

Education must change so as to reflect the prevailing industries and preoccupations of society.

To give you an overview of what's on offer at university – and what type of career future the different subjects can offer you – this chapter explores the following seven subject clusters:

- Business-related courses
- Social studies (including law)
- Medicine and health
- Sciences
- Modern languages
- Humanities
- Arts

Under each subject cluster you will discover what graduates from these degree courses have gone on to do in recent years, who's employed them, in what type of jobs they have started work and what level of starting salary they have averaged. But that's not all. To give you a better understanding of what it's like to be a graduate in these subject groupings, for each cluster we have case studies based on the experiences of recent graduates included.

Business

Subjects in this category can include:

- Accountancy
- Business studies
- Marketing
- Human resources
- Finance

Overview

No doubt about it, business is the new rock 'n' roll. Once, businesses were dour, uninspiring and locked in tradition. Now, thanks to companies like Apple, Virgin, Innocent Smoothie and Google, businesses attract their own fan base. Who did Sir Paul McCartney turn to when releasing his new album? Starbucks. When mocha becomes bigger than Macca, you know that a shift has really taken place.

Reasons to study these subjects

Business degrees have a very strong track record. Fawned over by employers and students alike, with over 4,500 courses on offer, the range of business-related courses on offer is immense. But it's not just about study. Business graduates are highly employable – in fact, they enjoy some of the highest levels of employment of any degree discipline – and business courses lead to a broad range of jobs and careers. This is partly because business courses bring with them commercial awareness – an essential skill sought after by thousands of recruiters. Many business courses also include in-built and accredited work experience (which can count towards your final grade). Together, commercial awareness and work experience equal a nearly unbeatable combination.

Career destinations

Because of their strong work focus, business degrees can lead to an extensive range of careers. In subjects like accountancy, strong links to the accountancy profession exist. In other business subjects, however, links to specific careers are less clear. But don't let this deter you. Graduates in business can be found in most careers, from banking to show business.

Business graduates are great entrepreneurs, good at running businesses. But despite this, relatively few (3.3%) choose to start their own companies directly after graduation. Instead, most choose to work for an employer, the most popular being retail. The retail sector remains the single biggest recruiter of business graduates, as is shown in Table 18. Companies like Aldi, Marks & Spencer, Sainsbury, Tesco and Arcadia each have their own two-year graduate management training programme.

Table 18: Top five job categories for business graduates
Source: AGCAS

	NUMBER OF GRADUATES RECRUITED	PERCENTAGE OF BUSINESS GRADUATES EMPLOYED
Retail	2,910	16.7%
Professional services	2,570	14.7%
Finance	2,205	12.6%
Hotel and accommodation	1,180	6.7%
Manufacturing	1,175	6.7%

Included with the permission of AGCAS and HESCU. For the latest version of this publication see www.prospects.ac.uk. For permission to reproduce, contact copyright@ agcas.org.uk and copyright@prospects.ac.uk.

The second most popular recruiter for this subject category is the professional services sector (human resources, management). This is followed by the financial services (banking, accountancy, investment banking and insurance). Even after the credit crunch, this sector remains very much the engine room of the UK economy, devouring business graduates in large quantities.

Following financial services are hotel and accommodation and manufacturing. As you can see, career variety is one of the key benefits of a business degree.

Show me the money!

Starting salaries for graduates of business-related courses are higher than the overall UK graduate average. At £21,607, finance graduates earn the highest salaries in this cluster (although this average tends to be inflated by the salaries paid by investment banks). According to the Association of Graduate Careers Advisory Services (AGCAS), business and management graduates also picked up above-average salaries (£19,985 and £20,622 respectively). Starting salaries for accountancy and marketing graduates were slightly lower – £18,971 and £18,546. But remember – these figures were recorded six months after graduation. Accountants, in particular, can expect significantly higher salaries after completing professional training contracts.

Business graduates are likely to earn higher starting salaries if their employer is a large organisation. Starting salaries can also be affected by where you live in the UK.

Points to consider

Business graduates are vocationally minded. This means that, compared to those from many other courses, they are more likely to leave university and go directly into the job market.

This partly explains why the unemployment figures for graduates from business courses can appear above average. The reason for this, however, is complex. Relatively few business graduates enrol for higher degrees, and they are generally either getting jobs or waiting to start jobs. This can make the unemployment figures for subjects in this cluster look higher than average, which may be misleading. Other subjects have lower unemployment figures because far more of their graduates stay on for postgraduate study.

But despite their popularity with employers, business graduates can't expect everything to go their way. For some jobs, even a degree in business is not enough. To be chartered accountant, for example, you will need to complete a professional training course. Most trainee accountants complete this on a part-time basis, alongside their accountancy day jobs. Small facts like these can have big impacts on destination statistics, for while 48.7% of accountancy graduates said they had secured jobs after university, another 24.4% said they were working *and* studying. If you combine data

Table 19: First destinations of UK graduates (2007–8) from business-related courses
Source: AGCAS

	NUMBERS GRADUATING	ENTERING EMPLOYMENT	ENTERING FURTHER STUDY	WORKING AND STUDYING	UNEMPLOYED AT TIME OF SURVEY	OTHER (%)
Accountancy	3,080	48.7%	7.8%	24.4%	10.9%	8.2%
Business courses	13,545	65.4%	7.5%	8.2%	8.9%	10.0%
Marketing	2,330	70.3%	5.0%	4.3%	9.6%	10.9%
All degree subjects	220,065	61.4%	14.1%	8.1%	7.9%	8.5%

Included with the permission of AGCAS and HESCU. For the latest version of this publication see www.prospects.ac.uk. For permission to reproduce, contact copyright @agcas.org.uk and copyright@prospects.ac.uk.

from the two columns in Table 19, you will see that accountancy actually produces the highest level of employment in the category (73.1%).

Forget the hype

As we have seen, graduates of business courses are highly employable, but, as competition for jobs intensifies, even a degree in such a vocational subject as this will not be enough to guarantee you a job unless you take serious steps to obtain lots of work experience (ideally as part of your course). You will also need to make sure that, while on the course, you take every opportunity to network with visiting speakers, employers and industry representatives.

If these subjects were a car they would be

A Volvo: rugged, reliable, and equipped with lots of practical uses. The downside is there are lots of them around.

Case study: Josh

Josh graduated in 2008 with a first in Business Studies. He found the course challenging, particularly the marketing modules which he chose to study in his second and final year. Like many business courses, Josh's degree included a six-month work placement, which he spent working in the finance department of a local manufacturing firm. The experience proved useful. Not only did it give him a first-hand insight into how businesses operate, it helped him appreciate that a career in finance was not for him. 'I always thought I wanted to work in the world of high finance. But several weeks in this firm's accounts department made me realise that it wasn't me. But it was a good experience, all the same.'

During the summer prior to his final year, Josh's university careers service helped him to arrange a work placement with a local marketing firm. The firm specialised in designing marketing materials for predominantly small and medium-sized firms, and also worked extensively in the field of website design. The experience proved to be important in helping shape Josh's longer-term career ideas. 'It was fascinating to watch how a firm of just four people could be so creative and so driven. They would all sit in an open-plan room shouting out ideas and then working long hours on these fantastic designs. The energy levels were like nothing I had ever seen before. The problem was, they hardly ever took on graduates; and I realised that my skills weren't up to what they wanted, even with a degree.'

So Josh decided to stay on at university and enrol for a Master's degree in Marketing. He explains: 'The summer job with the design agency gave me a real motivation for marketing – the Master's course would, hopefully, give me a better idea of the theories of marketing while also making me more marketable to employers.'

While studying for his Master's degree, Josh arranged a work placement with his university's corporate communications team – the team responsible for handling all the university's marketing and promotional activities. The experience gave him an insight into how large organisations promote themselves to their different stakeholders.

Social sciences

Subjects in this category can include:

- Anthropology
- Archaeology
- Communication studies
- Cultural studies
- Demography
- Economics
- Geography
- International development
- International relations
- Law
- Politics
- Psychology
- Sociology
- Social work

Overview

Social sciences subjects focus on people and their interactions with society. They ask why societies function and how they impact on communities and individuals. Of all the subjects in this category, law and psychology are the most popular with students. Every year, around 10,000 students graduate in each of these two subjects (compared to just 5,000 each in sociology and economics).

The popularity of law and psychology can be explained partly by the fact that both are, to some extent, vocational subjects, ie they can lead to certain identifiable careers and professions. But, as you will see, this doesn't mean that a career in these professions is guaranteed. Where social sciences are concerned, things are rarely as straightforward as they seem.

Reasons to study these subjects

Social sciences offer a fascinating insight into human existence and why people (and societies) behave as they do. In terms of sheer interest-value and mental gymnastics, social science subjects offer a unique and often highly theoretical glimpse of the world. As such, they are ideal subjects if you enjoy an argument or find yourself looking at the world and asking 'Why?'

Career destinations

Levels of employment among social sciences graduates are not always as they might appear at first glance (Table 20). First-destination statistics can often make it seem as if levels of employment among these students are below average. This is not necessarily the case. Above-average numbers of social science graduates opt to stay in higher education and study for higher degrees. This is particularly the case for graduates in politics. In 2008, one in five politics graduates enrolled for a higher degree – 6% higher than the national 'all subject' average.

Table 20: First destinations of social sciences graduates in 2008
Source: AGCAS

	Employment	Further study	Working and studying	Unemployed	Other
Economics	53.1%	14.5%	12.9%	8.8%	10.7%
Geography	57.8%	19.1%	6.5%	6.4%	10.2%
Law	35.2%	40.0%	10.9%	5.5%	8.4%
Politics	54.7%	20.2%	6.7%	8.8%	9.7%
Psychology	59.0%	14.5%	10.4%	7.4%	8.8%
Sociology	62.7%	12.9%	7.0%	8.4%	9.0%
All degrees	61.4%	14.1%	8.1%	7.9%	8.5%

Included with the permission of AGCAS and HESCU. For the latest version of this publication see www.prospects.ac.uk. For permission to reproduce, contact copyright @agcas.org.uk and copyright@prospects.ac.uk.

By far the highest level of further study, however, was recorded by law. In 2008, 40% of law graduates, remained in higher education – in most cases, to complete professional legal training courses (in order to become a solicitor or barrister, further legal study is mandatory).

Unemployment among social sciences graduates is roughly in line with the national average. Politics and economics recorded the highest levels of unemployment in this category: in both cases, unemployment was only one percentage point above the UK average.

Show me the money!

Chances are, you don't study social science subjects if your objective is to become rich. An analysis of Higher Education Statistics Agency (HESA) salary data shows that in 2008 the average starting salary for all UK graduates with first degrees was £20,763 for a 'graduate' job or £15,009 for a 'non-graduate job', and that among social science subjects there were widespread differences in earnings.

Table 21 shows that graduates of economics courses generally land the highest starting salaries, particularly when employed in graduate-level jobs. Economists out-earn psychologists by as much as £7,000 (or £4,000 when working in non-graduate jobs).

Table 21: **Starting salaries for 2008 social sciences graduates**
Source: HESA

Subject	Graduate employment or self-employment	Non-graduate employment or self-employment
Economics	£25,101	£17,316
Social work	£23,328	£15,572
Politics	£20,877	£15,364
Law	£19,805	£15,693
Social policy	£19,550	£14,079
Geography and environmental sciences	£19,545	£14,800
Anthropology	£19,485	£15,619
Sociology	£18,293	£14,528
Psychology	£18,091	£13,999
Total (all degree subjects)	£20,763	£15,009

Points to consider

Studying a social sciences subject will give you a broad range of skills and knowledge, but to boost your chances in the job market you must be ready to supplement your studies with work experience. Few social sciences courses come with this already in-built, which means that you may have to organise it for yourself. Your careers service will be able to advise you how to go about doing this.

Before enrolling on a social sciences degree course, ask your course tutors to supply you with information about what previous groups of students have gone on to do (it may also give you an idea of how career-friendly the course is).

Forget the hype

Remember: a degree in psychology will not guarantee you a job as a professional psychologist. These jobs are few and far between and increasingly require higher-level (ie postgraduate) degrees. If you want to work as a psychologist, make sure that your course is accredited by the British Psychological Society (BPS). If not, you may need to take special BPS-accredited 'conversion' courses, which could prove expensive.

If these subjects were a car they would be

An E-type Jaguar: classic design, great traditions and guaranteed to turn heads. But if you're going to reach your destination, be ready to put in lots of additional hours under the bonnet.

Case study: Claire

When Claire graduated with a degree in psychology, she had only one career aim in mind: occupational psychologist. During her degree course Claire had become very interested in different aspects of occupational

(Continued)

psychology – particularly those related to how organisations can use psychology to help them motivate their employees.

But as she entered her final year, Claire realised that jobs in occupational psychology rarely went to new graduates; instead, candidates with work experience and higher degrees were increasingly sought after. But Claire was adamant that postgraduate study was not for her – not yet, anyway. 'I just felt that I had been in education all my life and now was a time to do something different, to gain some experience outside of the classroom.'

After talking to her careers adviser she began to explore graduate training programmes, particularly those offered by some of the big retail firms. These were aimed specifically at graduates and were organised so that the first two years were spent training and gaining a first-hand insight into the business. After attending careers fairs and talks by firms in her university, Claire applied to several firms. The on-line application forms were lengthy and formidable; fortunately, however, she was offered several interviews and, during her final semester, was offered a job with a leading food retailer, on the company's graduate management programme.

Although Claire is not using her psychology degree directly, she takes a pragmatic view of the relationship between academic study and work: 'I'm not a psychologist – the word "psychologist" isn't in my job title – but in many ways I use my degree every single day at work. What psychology gives you is an understanding of how people behave, and how lots of different things affect this behaviour. As a trainee manager this is really helpful. I've been able to use my degree in writing training materials for new staff, even when giving advice to store managers about how best to set out their food displays. That's the great thing about psychology: you can use it all the time!'

Medicine and health

Subjects in this category can include:

• Medicine	• Speech therapy
• Dentistry	• Health science
• Physiotherapy	• Nursing
• Occupational therapy	• Public health

Overview

With the NHS retaining its position as the largest employer in the UK, opportunities for graduates in medicine and health-related subjects are set to remain buoyant. But while entry into medical and dentistry careers is tightly regulated by professional organisations, competition for jobs in other health-related fields has become considerably more competitive.

Reasons to study these subjects

Medical and health-related courses are vocational in the true sense of the word: they call for lots of dedication, commitment and almost selfless dedication to others. Graduates from these subjects are also very employable, enjoying some of the highest levels of employment in the UK.

Career destinations

Which career you choose to follow after graduation from these disciplines will depend to a large extent on your first degree. Medicine and dentistry graduates have almost 100% employment in their chosen fields. Health-related courses offer more diversity.

Of those graduating from health-related courses in 2007–08, 75% secured employment in health-related, professional occupations. Jobs included: physiotherapy trainee, nursing, radiography, health-service management and occupational therapy. Graduates in these subjects were also employed in jobs which involved personal services (eg human resources), education and professional management.

Show me the money!

Starting salaries for graduates from health-related courses are in line with national averages.

According to the NHS, junior doctors earn a basic salary and will usually be paid a supplement. In Foundation Year 1, a doctor will earn approximately £33,285. This increases in the second year to £41,285. A doctor in specialist training, on a 50% supplement, could earn from £44,117 to £69,369.

Salaried dentists who are employed by the NHS primary care trusts and who work mainly with community dental services earn between £37,344 and £79,875.

Points to consider

Gaining entry into medical and dentistry careers is extremely competitive. Not only will you need excellent academic qualifications and grades, you will also be expected to be able to demonstrate appropriate personal qualities. Once you have embarked on one of these courses, be prepared for several years of extremely hard work.

Each year roughly 6,000 students graduate in medicine and dentistry. Of these, almost all secure employment in their chosen fields within the first few months. Levels of unemployment among medicine and related subjects are less than 1%.

Applications to the NHS management training programme increased by 83% in 2009 – a sign that the UK's biggest employer is rapidly becoming one of its most popular.

Forget the hype

Most medicine graduates enter the medical profession via the two-year Foundation Programme. Once you have completed the first year of the programme you are formally registered with the General Medical Council (GMC). From this, most choose to specialise in a particular medical field. Of these, the vast majority are employed by the NHS.

For further information about opportunities in medicine and health-related courses, see the Graduate Prospects website (www.prospects. ac.uk), which contains lots of useful information and careers data, most of which has been written by university careers experts.

Even after such a focused degree programme, alternative career routes do exist. Every year a few medical graduates venture into non-medical jobs, such as management consultancy, lecturing and teaching. But for those graduates who do leave the profession, careers advisers suggest that most should still complete the first year of their Foundation Programme.

If these subjects were a car they would be

A Rolls Royce: traditional, expensive car, assembled by experts and esteemed by everyone. But if you want one, be prepared to put in years of hard work and dedication.

Sciences

Subjects in this category can include:

- Biology
- Chemistry
- Environmental science
- Physics

- Sports science
- Veterinary science
- Agriculture and related subjects

Overview

A degree in a science-related subject offers lots of scope for career development – and not just in scientific jobs. As this section will demonstrate, graduates from science courses are proving highly popular with employers. Why? Because not only do they offer hard-to-gain subject knowledge, their academic training also helps them to acquire a range of in-demand transferable skills. These include a practical and scientific approach to problem solving; strong research skills; the ability to communicate complex ideas and formulae (in easy to understand words); state of the art IT skills ... and they're good at maths. If you add to this the formula for employability (Work Experience + Strategies x Contacts) you're looking potentially at a winning combination.

Reasons to study these subjects

A degree in a science subject qualifies you for a broad range of careers – not just in a scientific field, but in other business and professional careers where the skills gained from science degree programmes are highly regarded.

Career destinations

The range of jobs in which science graduates are employed is broad, and which subject you choose to study will have a considerable impact on your future career. Nevertheless, despite the numbers of graduates in these subjects, relatively high numbers remain working in scientific and technical occupations.

Compared to those from many other subjects, science graduates are more likely to stay in education after graduation. Courses studied include

Master's degrees, professional diplomas and doctorates (PhD). Physics graduates, in particular, are more likely to remain in higher education. In 2008, more than a third (36%) of graduates from this subject enrolled for higher degrees (Table 22).

Table 22: First destinations of sciences graduates in 2008
Source: AGCAS

	EMPLOYMENT	FURTHER STUDY	WORKING AND STUDYING	UNEMPLOYED	OTHER
Biology	51.1%	24.3%	6.9%	9.2%	8.5%
Chemistry	44.0%	34.5%	6.0%	8.5%	7.0%
Environmental science	54.5%	20.4%	6.4%	8.6%	10.1%
Physics	37.9%	36.3%	8.5%	9.1%	8.2%
Sports science	61.2%	16.6%	8.0%	5.6%	8.6%
All subjects	61.4%	14.1%	8.1%	7.9%	8.5%

Included with the permission of AGCAS and HESCU. For the latest version of this publication see www.prospects.ac.uk. For permission to reproduce, contact copyright @agcas.org.uk and copyright@prospects.ac.uk.

In 2008, 31% of biology graduates started their careers in scientific and technical-related occupations. The figure for chemistry was even higher (41.3%).

Against this, just 2% of environmental science graduates entered scientific careers. Of these, 14% found work in technical and scientific jobs. Of the rest, 14% were employed as public and private sector managers – in doing so, proving the versatility of the subject.

The career destinations of physics graduates are even more interesting and counter-intuitive – they become finance specialists. It may come as a surprise to discover that physics graduates are less likely to work in scientific jobs than in business and finance (including accountancy). Fewer than 10% of physics graduates in 2008 found work in scientific, research and analysis occupations and just 7% were employed in engineering.

But almost double the number secured jobs in financial services (high-street banking, accountancy, insurance and investment banking).

Sports science graduates also enter a broad range of occupations. Again in 2008, almost a quarter of sports graduates began their careers as sports professionals. This included working in sports therapy, sports coaching and sports instructing. Eight per cent found work in business and finance and 12% enrolled for teacher training. Apart from their obvious love of sport, it seems that sports graduates are particularly good at working with people – not all of whom are clothed in tracksuits.

Show me the money!

Physics tends to generate the highest starting salaries. According to AGCAS, within just six months of graduation in 2008, graduates from this subject were averaging £22,291 (compared to the UK all-subject average of £19,677). This is likely to have something to do with physics graduates' on-going attraction into highly paid financial careers.

Average earnings for graduates of other science subjects were: chemistry: £20,392; biology: £17,376; environmental science: £17,762; and sports science: £16,627.

Points to consider

As the number of graduates leaving universities has increased, the value of a 'hard' science degree – particularly in chemistry and physics – has increased. Employers value graduates from scientific subjects for their analytical and technical skills. These are particularly in demand in sectors such as pharmaceuticals, scientific research and engineering.

Environmental science graduates are also increasingly in demand among energy firms, many of which are keen to demonstrate their green credentials.

You may be surprised at how many sports science graduates find employment in sports-related industries. Bear in mind, however, that many of these jobs are likely to be part time or fixed term.

Forget the hype

Not all graduates in science subjects start their careers in occupations that are in line with their qualifications. Six months after graduation, 13% of sports science and environmental science graduates were employed in clerical and secretarial jobs (compared to just 6% of chemists, and 9.9% of biologists).

If these subjects were a car they would be

A Porsche: admired by many, but notoriously complicated and difficult to master. Any momentary lack of concentration will find you veering wildly off track.

Case study: Jennifer

Jennifer's first degree was in chemistry – a subject which she had always loved while in school. She found the first year difficult; her degree course was highly theoretical and at times she found it hard to see how what she learned in the laboratory related to the world outside. Fortunately, her university had recently won the contract to deliver 'Shell Step' – a student internship programme which offered paid summer placements with local firms. Jennifer applied and was offered a place. Her placement involved carrying out lab-based research in a local chemical research company. Immediately, everything clicked! Not only could she apply her academic learning – she found that the company was very keen to learn from her – after all, she explains, her university work was cutting edge: 'It was amazing that they wanted to learn from me, not the other way around.'

(Continued)

Jennifer's placement went from strength to strength, and at the end of the summer she was entered for a regional competition to see which student had had the best placement experience. She won, and was recommended to apply for the national finals.

Looking back, Jennifer's experience has helped her to crystallise her career ideas. She now wants to remain in higher education to study for a PhD (subject to research council funding). After that, she sees her options as being either to work as a research chemist in industry or to become an academic.

Languages

Subjects in this category include

- French
- German
- Spanish
- Latin American studies
- Aramaic
- Celtic studies
- Chinese studies
- Classical Arabic
- Classical Greek studies

- Classical studies
- French studies
- Hebrew
- Irish Gaelic
- Italian studies
- Japanese studies
- Latin language
- Middle Eastern studies
- Portuguese

Overview

As the job market becomes ever more competitive, more students than ever have been enrolling on to language courses. The good news is that employers are very positive about the skills gained from language degrees.

Reasons to study these subjects

Language graduates are in demand across a range of sectors – retail, manufacturing, public sector (including all branches of the Civil Service), the media, advertising, communications and marketing. And because the take-up of foreign languages in schools has been declining in recent years, graduates with language skills are at a potential advantage.

Career destinations

Compared to UK averages, graduates from language courses are more likely to stay on in higher education after completing their first degree. Postgraduate courses taken by these graduates include: Master's degree in Translation, Property Valuation and Broadcast Journalism.

Language graduates also study for higher degrees in non-linguistic subjects, such as Information Technology, International Business, Master's in Business Administration (MBA) and Hospitality and Tourism.

As Table 23 shows, around one in five language graduates in 2008 worked in the education sector – but not all became teachers. In total, just 5% of language graduates went on to become teachers, while almost 6% enrolled for other study and training, including courses in professional translation.

Table 23: The top five job categories for language graduates
Source: AGCAS

INDUSTRIAL CLASSIFICATION	NUMBERS OF GRADUATES	PERCENTAGE
Education	1,880	20%
Retail	1,320	14%
Information and communication	820	9%
Professional occupations	855	9%
Manufacturing	285	3%

Included with the permission of AGCAS and HESCU. For the latest version of this publication see www.prospects.ac.uk. For permission to reproduce, contact copyright @agcas.org.uk and copyright@prospects.ac.uk.

Another 6.6% of language graduates began their careers in lecturing posts. In most cases, these were in further education (in which formal teacher training qualifications are not required). Some of these posts were part time. This illustrates an important point: a degree in languages can offer you a range of options, including teaching or lecturing.

Relatively few graduates from language courses began their careers in translation and interpretation. These jobs tend to call for experience and further professional training. As such, new graduates are rarely hired direct from university.

Relatively few language graduates work in jobs where they spend their days communicating in their specialist languages. Nevertheless, the fact that they have acquired such excellent communication skills makes them highly employable. Above average numbers of language graduates start their careers working in public and private sector management, where they are employed in jobs as diverse as human resources manager, retail management trainee and financial adviser.

Language graduates are also employed in business and financial careers – two sectors in which high-level communication skills are essential. In 2008, slightly fewer than 12% of graduates from these subjects were recruited directly after university to work in these fields. It's an incredible to think that more language graduates began their careers in banking and accountancy than in translation and interpretation!

Show me the money!

The average starting salary for (European) language graduates in 2008 was approximately £19,000.

Points to consider

Education remains the single most popular recruiter of language graduates (although not all jobs will be in teaching and lecturing). Following this are jobs in retail, information and communication, professional occupations and manufacturing. If manufacturing sounds a strange occupation for language graduates, it can be explained by the fact that many manufacturers with overseas contracts to fulfil recruit linguists in order to communicate with overseas clients.

Forget the hype

Non-graduate jobs are an occupational hazard for language graduates. In 2008, six months after graduation, 17% of language graduates were employed in clerical and secretarial jobs. A further 12% were employed in retail and bar work. In some of these jobs graduates will no doubt move on to other careers. Nevertheless, it appears that, for now, under-employment for these graduates remains a greater threat than unemployment.

If these subjects were a car they would be

An Alfa Romeo: looks and sounds great, but requires lots of specialist knowledge and the ability to understand complicated instructions written in a foreign language.

Humanities

Subjects in this category can include:

- English
- History
- Media studies

Overview

What can you do with a degree in english, or history, or media studies? Every year, at university open days up and down the country, admission tutors are bombarded by this question. So what can you do with a humanities degree – apart from teaching?

Reasons to study these subjects

Students study these subjects for a variety of reasons, eg love of the subject and an intention to pursue it professionally. But opportunities in careers related to humanities subjects are difficult to find – particularly without prior work experience. Yet, far from this being a barrier to employment, many employers from a broad range of sectors look to graduates from these subjects as future managers. The question is: is this how humanities graduates view their future careers?

Career destinations

According to HESA, the largest single job category for humanities graduates is education. But this doesn't always mean teaching. Humanities graduates work across the education sector in a wide and complex range of jobs. These include: educational administrators, managers, HR professionals and finance officers.

The second-largest recruiter of humanities graduates is the retail sector. Nationally, retail is a huge recruiter of graduates. Humanities graduates are recruited to work at all levels within retail organisations and are among the most likely to be recruited as retail management trainees.

The public sector is the third-biggest recruiter, hiring around 9% of the overall national total. Again, this sector is extremely complex and covers a broad range of occupations, from social workers to HR professionals.

Graduates in humanities like being students. In fact, there is an above-average tendency for graduates in this category to remain in higher education and to enrol for further and higher qualifications. Roughly one in five of graduates with english and history degrees enrol for postgraduate study, as compared to just 6% of media studies graduates. Many of these courses are at Master's level, examples being Women's Studies, English Literature, 19th Century Literature and Egyptology. Above average numbers of students from these subjects also enrol for doctoral-level study, although in recent years obtaining funding for such studies has proved increasingly difficult.

Postgraduate teacher training is a popular option among english graduates. In 2008, 6.4% of english graduates enrolled for Postgraduate Certificate in Education (PGCE) courses, compared to just 3.6% of those graduating in history, and just 1.6% in media studies.

One of the reasons why many graduates from english degrees enrol for postgraduate study could be linked to the difficulties students experience when trying to find their niche in the job market. In 2008, some 7% of english graduates started their careers in marketing-related jobs (eg account executive, PR manager), while a similar proportion were employed as public or private sector management trainees. But these tended to be the exceptions. English graduates were no more likely to be unemployed than graduates in any other subject. Under-employment, however, remains an ever-present risk. Just over 18% of english graduates reported their first job after university as being in clerical or secretarial work, while a further 17% said they were working in retail (non-management level) or low-level catering and hospitality work.

History graduates have marginally more options. Compared to english, fewer history graduates enrolled for postgraduate study. As a result, more entered the job market. Eleven per cent of history graduates were employed in public or private sector management and slightly fewer than 9% were working in business and financial careers (there is evidence of historians being employed as trainee accountants, trainee auditors and investment bankers).

For historians too, under-employment remained a concern. Roughly 19% of graduates in this subject began work in administrative and secretarial jobs, while another 17% found themselves in retail and catering jobs.

Perhaps unfairly, it is the destinations of media studies graduates which every year provoke the greatest national discussion. Often, media coverage of media studies is extremely negative. Journalists, such as the BBC's John Humphrys, waste no opportunities to complain that they would never employ a graduate in media studies – preferring instead to hire only those with 'traditional' academic degrees. This is unfair. It also ignores the fact that education must change so as to reflect the prevailing industries and preoccupations of society. Some of the highest-paid executives in broadcasting and news media are media studies graduates.

According to What do graduates do? recent media graduates began work as runners, researchers, production assistants, junior editors and quality controllers.

Show me the money!

Salaries for graduates in humanities subjects, according to AGCAS, ranged from £16,295 for media studies and £16,642 for English. For other subjects, the average was approximately £19,600.

Points to consider

Compared to media studies, twice as many students graduate each year in english and history. But despite its somewhat controversial reputation – in the media, of all places – media studies produces among the highest levels of employment in the UK. That's the good news. With media studies, there's always a catch. Graduates in this subject are also among the most likely to be unemployed.

Forget the hype

Because they are less likely to be represented on postgraduate courses, media studies graduates have both higher than average levels of unemployment and greater representation in non-graduate jobs. One in five media studies graduates began their career after university in retail or catering jobs, while a further 15% reported that they were working in clerical or secretarial jobs.

If these subjects were a car they would be

A Morris Minor: adored by aficionados, but looked on with confusion and perplexity by others.

Creative arts

Subjects in this category can include:

- Art and design
- Contemporary arts
- Clothing design
- Dance
- Drama
- Fine arts
- Graphics
- Industrial design
- Interior design
- Music
- Performing arts
- Photography
- Web design

Overview

In recent years there has been a 12% increase in the number of graduates leaving universities with creative arts degrees.

For the next two decades, opportunities in the creative sector are widely predicted to expand. Relative to its GDP, the UK has the largest cultural economy in the world, employing 678,480 people and contributing £24 billion towards the UK economy. One estimate predicts that the creative industries will require an additional 150,000 people by 2017. According to the Department for Business, Innovation and Skills, much of this growth will be consumed by the digital and creative.

Reasons to study these subjects

In recent years there has been a 12% increase in the number of graduates leaving university with creative arts degrees.

For the next two decades, opportunities in the creative sector are widely predicted to expand. Relative to its GDP, the UK has the largest cultural economy in the world, employing 678,480 people and contributing £24 billion towards the UK economy. One estimate predicts that the creative industries will require an additional 150,000 people by 2017.

Career destinations

Graduates in art and design are less likely than those from other subjects to enrol for postgraduate study (Table 24). At the same time, graduates in these subjects can experience above-average levels of unemployment. But within this category, differences exist. Unemployment, for example, is lower among performing arts graduates, who, in turn, are twice as likely as those in art and design to enrol for further study.

Table 24: First destinations of creative arts graduates
Source: HESA

	EMPLOYMENT	FURTHER STUDY	WORKING AND STUDYING	UNEMPLOYED	OTHER
Art and design	64.6%	7.0%	5.2%	12.2%	11.0%
Performing arts	62.4%	14.5%	7.5%	7.9%	7.7%
All subjects	61.4%	14.1%	8.1%	7.9%	8.5%

Almost a quarter (23%) of performing arts graduates secured jobs in creative industry occupations. These can include acting, directing, arts administration and tutoring. An additional 13% are employed in education-related jobs – coaching, lecturing, drama teaching. Some of these jobs are likely to be freelance – meaning that, in effect, the graduate is self-employed. Just over 4% of performing arts graduates enrol directly for a postgraduate teaching programme.

Show me the money!

According to What do graduates do? (AGCAS, 2009) average starting salaries for graduates from creative arts courses are among the lowest in the sector, ranging from £14,843 for fine arts graduates to £16,469 for design students.

Nationally, 62% of those employed in creative industries earn less than £20,000; while one in 10 earn more than £41,000.

But remember: these are starting salaries. Creative arts graduates will tell you that even for the most talented – and connected – it can take several years to become established in your chosen field. After that, for some, the opportunities can be dazzling.

Points to consider

What employers look for from creative arts graduates is a combination of skills and experience. The creative sector is also an industry in which contacts can play a decisive role. Unfortunately, however, work experience in the creative sector can come at a cost. Because employers recognise and understand the importance of work experience for creative graduates' careers, many are not prepared to pay their interns. This state of affairs seems unlikely to end any time soon. The credit crunch and the squeeze for jobs have actually multiplied the number of unpaid internships being offered in the creative sector.

Forget the hype

Although the creative sector is expanding, many jobs are part time in small (and even micro) organisations. As such, 'traditional' career paths can be few and far between. Be ready to have a Plan B – even if it lasts for a number of years until you have developed the skills, experience and contacts to progress your creative career. Being geographically mobile can also help. Almost a fifth of creative jobs are located in London.

If these subjects were a car they would be

A Ferrari: great design, looks terrific, but can be highly expensive and, let's face it, it's not exactly practical.

E =
Employability,
Q =
Qualifications,
WE = Work
Experience,
S = Strategies
and
C = Contacts

Work Experience

$$E = Q + \textbf{\textit{WE}} + S \times C$$

"I have no special talent. I am only passionately curious."

Albert Einstein

Chapter 8

Work experience

It is now widely recognised that work experience is the key to employability. But what is it – and why is it so effective?

Why work experience?

No matter how well you do in your academic studies, when 400,000 degree holders graduate from universities every year, qualifications alone are not enough to guarantee employability. For this, you need *work experience*.

Experts have long recognised that work experience can play a vital role in helping enhance your employability. As we saw in Section 2, students whose degree courses include 'sandwich' placements (periods of organised work experience built into their course curriculum) often have considerably higher levels of employment than those whose courses don't provide this experience.

It's not difficult to see why work placements are so popular with employers. Not only do they help to develop additional work-related skills and knowledge; by forming a bridge between academic theory and work-based practice, they can even make you a better student.

Developing key employability skills

'In the current economic climate, it is essential that graduates are prepared to enter the workplace possessing key employability skills which will enable them to compete in today's job market. Universities and employers both have an important role to play in providing work placements, internships and opportunities which can assist in the development of these skills, such as campus talks from employers and specific employability modules.'

CBI, Future Fit, 2009

Not only are students who go on work placements more marketable than those who don't; on graduation many of them are hired by the very organisations where they had their work placements. When it comes to work experience, it seems that everyone is a winner: students, academics and, of course, employers.

The problem is that there are never enough sandwiches to go around. Those that do exist tend to be unevenly distributed among vocational subjects, particularly those in engineering and science-related disciplines.

This creates a self-fulfilling prophecy: degree subjects with lower levels of employment (ie arts and humanities) rarely include sandwich placements. Students in these subjects can therefore be doubly disadvantaged. Not only do they study subjects with comparatively lower levels of employment; the way these courses are organised means that many students graduate without the experience required by employers.

As the benefits of work experience are becoming more widely understood, this situation has been gradually changing. Across universities as a whole, there is now much greater awareness of the advantages of work experience – particularly for students of non-vocational subjects. More universities are also experimenting with sandwich-style placements; others are looking at ways of accrediting work experience so that it actually counts towards students' degree classification.

This chapter and the next one take a closer look at work experience – what it is (and isn't), how it works, the type of work experience opportunities available at most universities, and why, suddenly, everyone is talking about internships.

Measuring the benefits

Employers are unequivocal in their enthusiasm for work experience – but only if it the experience is managed in a professional and effective manner. In other words, you need to be absolutely clear, before embarking on the experience, about what you want to gain from the experience and how it will make you a better prospective employee. The differences between students who have had relevant work experience and those who haven't are often stark.

> **Placement checklist**
>
> A quality work placements gives you:
>
> ✓ Clear aims and objectives
> ✓ On-going support
> ✓ New learning
> ✓ Personal development
> ✓ Assessment

The rise of work experience comes at a time when more employers are questioning the value of academic qualifications. As the National Centre for Work Experience (NCWE) argues, 'Employers accept that it is no longer sufficient to have a good degree classification alone. Employers are increasingly looking for students who can demonstrate employability competencies such as business acumen, professionalism and communication skills.'

In a study undertaken as part of the Real Prospects survey, entitled *Why work experience matters! Real Prospects 2009 graduates' experiences of placements, internships and work experience*, author Kathrine Jensen attempts to identify the main benefits linked to work

> ❝ According to the CBI, 82% of employers want universities to commit more time and resources to improving students' employability skills. For many, this means increasing opportunities for students to engage in work experience. ❞

experience. These include: the development of skills and attitudes, help with shaping ideas about future careers, giving students an insight into office life, and an opportunity to build and develop contacts. In addition to this list, she cites another strategic benefit that has hitherto rarely been acknowledged: work experience can lead to job offers.

Short cut to a job

Researchers working on Real Prospects were surprised by the high numbers of graduates who claimed that either during or after their work experience they had been encouraged by the employer to apply for future jobs with the organisation. Some had even been offered contracts of employment. In some cases, contacts created during the placement had led to the students being able to short-cut some of the standard application procedures. Others claimed that the work experience had given them a significant advantage when competing with other graduates.

Several students were quoted in Jensen's research paper, which discussed their work experience placements.

> I had worked here for a year as part of my degree (industrial placement year) and therefore I had previous knowledge of the company and many contacts. I was informed of the position before graduation and therefore applied and secured the job before completing my course.

> My current employment is the result of an extended work experience position, which led on to the creation of a job role within the company. I got the work experience because I had inkling that I would like to work within publishing and a colleague informed me that she knew someone who could probably get me a little experience. I had no interview etc, I just e-mailed and got a placement. When I was there, I made myself known and I made myself necessary.

> My employer found me as part of an application I made through an internship scheme. I worked for them for a summer and at the end of that time they offered me a full time post for the following September once I had completed my studies.

> After completing a voluntary internship with the employer, I was made aware of their vacancies at the time, one of which, higher members of the organisation strongly suggested I apply for. I felt very comfortable with the working environment having grown quite accustomed to it during my internship and was made to feel very welcome throughout.

K. Jensen, Why work experience matters! Real Prospects 2009 graduates' experiences of placements, internships and work experience, (2009).

Experience your own future

Work experience also provides you with a first-hand opportunity to gain an insight into a particular organisation or sector. It's also very effective in giving you an understanding of the informal or 'invisible' aspects of business life – the cultures, traditions and unspoken laws which shape all organisations. If used correctly, this information can easily become first-hand intelligence, which you can use to help shape your future career plans. As one graduate in the Real Prospects research was quoted as saying,

> After completing a one year industrial placement with my current employer, I knew that the career opportunities presented were exactly what I wanted. The job offers so much diversity in terms of the day-to-day tasks and the people. My employer is also a globally recognised company, which provided a lot of impetus for me to apply.

Getting to know you

One of the main benefits of work experience is its capacity to help you make contacts with people in work — contacts which may eventually give you an insight into a particular job or even lead you to particular opportunities.

> ❝ I did a placement year working for a similar company and got to know the names of competitors. Through searching the websites of other companies and the areas they specialise in I decided to join a company with a similar structure to that of my placement year company. ❞

A number of students in Jensen's work experience study gave examples of how a temporary work experience position had led to a paid job. On one occasion, a student had been offered a job on the strength of her work experience alone. Neither an application nor an interview were deemed necessary.

Chapter 14 looks at how the contacts made through work experience can be used to build a powerful career network.

From work experience to full-time job

'I started as a temp in an internal department and liked being able to move around within the local government structure. When I finished at university there was a temp to permanent opening which I took in order to save for a postgraduate degree. After 3 months I was offered a full time, permanent contract working with two different teams, neither of which required an application form or an interview as the posts were specifically tailored to suit me and the tasks given to me to complete.'

The six-month interview

But the benefits of work experience are not stacked entirely on the student's side. Recruiters themselves are increasingly viewing work experience as an opportunity to check out the best graduates. Some are even going as far as to hire only graduates who have had work experience with their organisation. This has major implications for the future of graduate recruitment; it should also be a wake-up call to you. If major recruiters are now switching to hiring-via-placements, you need to ensure that you use your time at university wisely, and make sure that you take the issue of work experience very seriously. Literally speaking, your career could depend on it.

Because student placements are relatively inexpensive for recruiters, they represent an excellent return on investment when and if the company should choose to recruit a placement student after graduation. And placements are not only relatively cheap: by creating links between university departments, students and tutors, they also offer organisations an opportunity to gain access to the latest academic thinking and research. (The alternative is hiring an expensive consultancy firm!)

Placements also offer a company an extended period of time in which to assess your skills, motivation, values and commitment (in other words, all the skills listed above). What better way to assess how motivated you are than by assessing your time-keeping over a period of six-months in a real-life work setting?

Finally, recruiting graduates after they have left university is both expensive (in terms of higher salaries) and riskier (there's no guarantee that a new graduate will stay the course, or not be poached by another firm). Recruitment via placement students therefore represents good business practice — as the Godfather, Don Corleone, might have put it, hiring a student from a work placement represents an offer few employers can refuse.

From placement to hiring

According to Graduate Prospects (www.prospects.ac.uk), your chances of being hired by your placement provider once you have graduated are approximately one in three.

'In 2008 we took on 150 graduates. One year on, the table has dropped to 50. But placements are a different story. In 2008 we offered 230 placements. This year, that number has increased to 300. This is a tactical shift. We now see placements as a "one-year interview"'.

Graduate Recruitment Manager, major US blue-chip computing firm

---

It's true. Between 20% and 30% of placement students are offered graduate jobs by the companies and organisations for which they work. This proves that work placements are the most effective route into graduate-level employment.

Product testing

So what makes for a good work placement?

According to Graduate Prospects, quality work placements should provide you with a set of clearly laid-out objectives (in other words, what you aim to achieve during the placement), support from both your university department and the organisation itself, new learning, opportunities for personal development and a way of measuring or assessing what you have learned from the experience.

Placement providers should also be able to demonstrate senior commitment and strategies for the intern programme. Companies that have been awarded the NCWE Quality Mark have demonstrated that they met a national standard of work experience provision. Students carrying out placements at these organisations can be confident that they will receive a structured and worthwhile placement.

Developing employability skills

'The importance of employability skills is now greater than ever in the
current economic climate. Work placements are one way of providing
a means by which these skills can be attained. We have seen the results
and the value of this firsthand not just for Centrica but also for the
valuable skills development that students experience while with us. In
order to be well prepared for the upturn, we need to ensure that we are
producing graduates with higher level skills and the employability skills
which employers value in order to support the economy and meet the
needs of business.'

Sam Laidlaw, CEO of Centrica plc,

Universities now offer many types of work experience – from part-time
work to work-based shadowing. However, in recent years, curriculum-
based placements and longer 'internships' are fast becoming the most
popular options. These are more regulated and fit in alongside your
academic learning. In some courses, you can also gain academic credits
for your placements.

Although employers are responsive to a range of placement offers, those
that involve a link-up with a particular academic subject or discipline
tend to be the most popular. For example, some large firms have an
established track record of recruiting placement students from marketing
and human resources degree courses. In cases such as these, the career
and employability benefits to students are considerable.

But it's not only employability skills that can benefit from a work placement. Research has shown that students' academic skills are often
enhanced by a period in a work placement. Skills such as report writing,
giving presentations, time management and working in teams can all be
boosted by a spell outside of the lecture theatre. It can also help to firm
up – or radically alter – your career plans.

Types of work experience

Depending on the structure of your degree course, you can choose from a wide range of work placements. These include the following:

- **Placements and internships:** formal, structured programmes which may serve as a 'foot in the door'

- **Casual work experience:** informal, found by speculative applications or through contacts

- **Temporary work:** a chance to earn money and gain experience at the same time

> 66 Graduates have got to have work experience, but not just any type of work experience. I want to see people whose work experience is relevant to my firm. Something that proves that they're motivated and committed – that they've made a serious effort to get to know what we do. 99
>
> Graduate recruitment manager, retail

- **Voluntary work:** another great way to boost your skills base, particularly if you're pursuing a related career

- **Work shadowing:** unpaid, but can be the only option in some of the more competitive career areas

- **On-campus work:** your university will offer lots of opportunities for students to gain work experience, ranging from part-time jobs in the students' union to more formal positions in university departments and services

Work placement providers

Although universities and courses have their own guidelines on when work experience can take place, the majority of internships and placements happen in the summer before your final year at university. Year-long placements generally occur during the penultimate year of a sandwich degree course.

And it's not only the major organisations that offer placements. Small and medium-sized firms view work placements as an excellent opportunity to establish links with higher education, and for that reason are always worthwhile considering – even though few small firms enjoy the same level of visibility as the leading recruiters. Although few small firms will be able to offer you the level of support and access to resources that can be found in large organisations, they do have one major advantage – they can give you large amounts of responsibility, often from day one.

Getting paid

Average pay scales for work placements are notoriously difficult to estimate. One estimate states that while some larger firms pay students £23,000 for a year spent in industry, the sector-wide average is around £14,000. Relatively few work placements pay students less than £10,000 a year, and on the whole, while in the workplace you can expect to earn between £150 and £250 per week.

Pay for placements that take place during long vacations varies; large companies usually offer competitive packages of up to £300 per week.

Applying for placements and internships

With all the benefits attributed to work placements, it's not surprising that competition for popular work experience providers is just as intense as it is for graduate jobs. When selecting placement students, employers are no less rigorous than when selecting graduate recruits.

For some employers, the route into work placements closely mirrors that pursued when hiring graduates – with lengthy applications, first and second interviews, psychometric tests and even, with some firms, assessment centres. Typically, you are assessed against a range of aptitudes. Examples of these are:

> Work placements are all about who you know, and who knows you. If you're worried that you don't know anyone who might be able to lead you to a placement opportunity, don't worry. Your careers service and departmental tutors are there for that very purpose.

- Enthusiasm
- Maturity
- Determination
- Interpersonal skills (such as teamwork)

So where do you start? Below is a checklist for how to go about organising a work placement while at university. Remember, you don't have to go it alone: your tutors and your university careers service will be on hand at every stage to ensure that you are accessing all the support and resources available.

- **Know yourself:** What can you offer a prospective placement provider – academic skills, knowledge, relevant experience, lots of enthusiasm and motivation? If you don't know, you can't expect an employer to take the time to discover it. Write a list of what you're best at – if you're feeling modest, ask a friend to do it for you.

- **The rounded you:** No placement provider wants to spend large swathes of their work time with one-dimensional geeks; instead, they want to hire placement students who have lots to offer – in terms of academic skills and knowledge, and extracurricular activities.

So what else – beyond your A level grades and prize-winning assignments – can you offer? Remember, commitment to sports, activities, clubs and societies can all be used effectively to promote a rounded personality.

- **Your experiences:** What have you done in your life so far that can illuminate your application form? What holiday or part-time jobs have you had (and from these, what skills and attributes have you gained)? Have you participated in any previous work experience? What about representing your school or college? As a student, have you participated in any extracurricular competition, eg the Global Management Challenge (for more information, see www.gmc.hobsons.co.uk)? Employers are particularly keen to see motivated and committed applicants, so even if a previous experience hasn't gone particularly well, you can always turn things round by describing what you have learned from the experience. What might you do differently next time – and how has the experienced changed your outlook?

- **See yourself from the employer's point of view:** Applying for work placements isn't all about what you want: you also need to focus on the placement provider's needs. These are usually listed in the information material accompanying the application form. If not, you might find it on the company website. If all else fails, contact your careers adviser or tutor. Whatever happens, never send in an application without being able to offer your potential provider something in return – skills, knowledge, personal attributes or simply a willingness to make the tea.

- **No waffle – evidence!** Once you have made a list of all the skills and experience you are offering your potential placement provider, the next thing you need to do is to draw up a list of all the skills you need but currently don't have. Before finishing the list, make sure that your examples are as comprehensive as possible; recruiters like to see that you have experienced a range of different situations, so be ready to think of several examples for each skill.

- **Contacts:** Work placements are all about who you know, and who knows you. If you're worried that you don't know anyone who might be able to lead you to a placement opportunity, don't worry. Your careers service and departmental tutors are there for that very purpose. But the chances are, you do have some leads – usually closer to hand than you realise (for more on this, see Chapter 14 on contacts and networking). Start by drawing up a list of the kinds of environments in which you would like to have a placement; then, once a picture is beginning to emerge, try to think of organisations that operate within these sectors. Careers libraries are excellent resources for this, as are websites such as those listed on page 225.

- **Location, location, location:** No matter how exciting a placement sounds, you have to be practical. For most students, location plays as much a part in a placement's success or failure as any other factor. How far are you able/willing to travel for your placement – and where will you live? What budget is available to you –and how long is it likely to last? Tip: from a budgetary perspective, staying with friends and relatives for the duration of a work placement is always the best idea.

- **Timescale:** For this you will need to consult extensively with your course tutor. Whenever you decide to take your work placement, you must be absolutely certain that it does not conflict with your academic studies (damaging your degree prospects is the ultimate in counter-productive career strategies). Your course tutor will be able to advise you on this. Listen very carefully.

- **Assessment:** How will you know if your placement has been a success? Can you gain academic credits for being on a work placement, and if so, how might that work? Even without credits, you will need to be sure, before starting a placement, about what it is you intend to get from the experience. Only then can you be certain that the placement will be a success.

- **Networks:** Finally, who is in your support network – who are the people who will support you while you are on placement? Think of them as your Grand Prix team, the people who will dust you down, help you refuel and monitor your performance. Being on work placement can at times be a lonely and extremely challenging experience – having people on hand in the placement organisation, or just at the end of a telephone line, can make all the difference.

E = Employability,
Q = Qualifications,
WE = Work Experience,
S = Strategies and
C = Contacts

Strategies

$$E = Q + WE + \textbf{S} \times C$$

"Insanity is doing the same things over and over again and expecting different results."

Albert Einstein

Chapter 9

Recruiters' strategies

The 'dialogue' between students and recruiters is starting to change.

3

An intensifying race

Ever since Usain Bolt exploded on to the world scene, the performances of other leading sprinters have been improving. They have had no choice. Simply in order to stay in the same camera shot as Bolt, every leading sprinter in the world has to go back to the drawing board to find a way of running faster and better than before. And as they have done so, the parameters of possibility have started to shift.

In the first-ever recorded example of reverse alchemy, Usain Bolt managed to turn a 2008 gold medal performance into a 2009 silver medal performance; and since then every athlete in the world has had to up his game. A similar phenomenon is occurring in the graduate job market.

> ## Bolt!
>
> 16 August 2009, men's 100m final, World Athletics Championship, Olympic Stadium, Berlin.
>
> Under the glare of the arc lights, Jamaican sprinter Usain Bolt prepares himself for the most important race of his life. Bolt already holds several world records, including that for the 100m, which he won in 2008 at the Beijing Olympics. His explosive speed and media-friendly persona have already made him one of the most famous athletes in the world.
>
> In Lane 5 is American sprint champion Tyson Gay. Like Bolt, he too has won multiple gold medals; he too is a winner. With little or no head wind, conditions in the Olympic Stadium are near perfect. Experts are predicting a desperately close finish.
>
> But what happens next will change history.
>
> With the boom of the starter's pistol still echoing in the stadium, Bolt powers down the track in an incredible 9.58 seconds. Not only is this 0.11 seconds faster than the time he set in Beijing, it represents the greatest single improvement in the men's 100-metres since 1968 – the year that electronic timing began.
>
> Almost unnoticed, Tyson Gay comes in second. Compared to Bolt, he looked as if he were out for a jog. His time, however, reveals a different

story. Not only has Gay just broken Bolt's 2008 world record – an achievement which, less than 10 seconds earlier would have made him the fastest sprinter in the world – he has just become America's greatest ever sprinter. And he still lost.

In any other year, Tyson Gay would have been the new world champion: the fastest human in history. But this was not any other year.

2009 was the year that the race suddenly got faster.

Running faster to stand still

As with professional athletes, today's students and graduates are discovering that if they want a chance of beating the competition, they too need to find ways of improving their performances, of upping their game.

> **The challenge isn't getting new ideas into your head; it's getting the old ideas out.**
>
> Seth Godin, marketing guru

Once, a university degree would have all but guaranteed this. Now, as we have seen, unless your degree is accompanied by relevant and appropriate work experience, your employability will be severely limited. Not that there is any particular mystery behind this. As in professional sprinting, a new era of rampant talent inflation is opening, and graduates are finding themselves at the forefront. As thousands of university leavers are again about to discover, skills, aptitudes, achievements and knowledge that once would have led to offers of jobs today don't even get you to first-interview stage.

If you want a chance to succeed in this environment, you too will have to go back to the drawing board and acquire new skills and tactics. This will mean rethinking much of what you currently take for granted about what it takes to get a job.

This and the next two chapters explore the strategies you will need if you are to have a chance of landing the job of your dreams. As the competition for graduate jobs hots up, these strategies will become even more crucial. To put it simply, there's no point in having an excellent degree and superb work experience if you don't have the skills and tactics at your command to make use of them.

Changing recruitment practices

According to a survey by AGR into recruitment practices, in all industries and sectors, levels of competition for 'graduate' jobs are on the rise. At the same time, under the influence of new internet technology, rising numbers of graduates and the need to cut costs, employers' recruitment practices are evolving – in some cases, radically.

Put yourself in the shoes of a graduate recruitment manager. Every year, as soon as you advertise your graduate vacancies, you are deluged with hundreds, even thousands of applications. Few of these applications really stand out; most offer similar levels of experience, similar qualifications and similar levels of commitment. So how are you going to choose between all these applicants?

The answer is: weapons of mass rejection.

Weapons of mass rejection

As the 'war for talent' has intensified, recruiters are increasingly looking at new ways of processing job applications – which, as we have seen, for some organisations each year run into the thousands. Fortunately for them, help is at hand. Their real name is **Employers' recruitment practices are evolving – radically.** psychometric assessments and inventories. Graduates should think of them as 'weapons of mass rejection'.

Weapons of mass rejection – or WMRs – is a nickname used here to describe these assessments. The primary aim of a WMR is to ensure that the organisation hires only the most suitable candidates for its graduate recruitment programme. The second aim is to ensure that every other applicant is rejected as swiftly and as efficiently as possible.

Some WMRs have been deployed by recruiters for years. Others are relatively new. Many have been made possible only by the invention of the internet, which more than any other technology is changing the graduate market.

Current examples of WMRs include:

- Electronic screening to assess application forms
- 'Psychometric' cognitive tests and 'IQ' assessments
- On-line personality, verbal reasoning and numeracy tests
- Enhanced use of telephone screening (often by external consultants or specialist call centres)
- Electronic 'motivation' questionnaires, designed to assess motivation and business awareness
- Group interviews and assessments
- Assessment centres

Typically, larger graduate recruiters with the necessary resources and trained staff have tended to deploy the greatest range of WMRs. However, as internet techniques have become cheaper, increasing numbers of small and medium-sized firms have started to use them.

For recruiters, WMRs offer an apparently failsafe response to rising numbers of applications; they are also relatively cheap (significantly cheaper than employing teams of HR professionals). And because most WMRs are concerned with measuring 'objective' competencies and skills, they avoid accusations of bias (although several academic studies have been published that question this assertion).

Note: Some WMRs are run by specially trained in-house company trainers; others are run by external consultants, although in recent years there has been a tendency for some larger employers to out-source this side of their recruitment and selection activity to external consultants.

The speed with which graduate recruiters have adopted WMRs has taken many people by surprise. Table 25 reveals how, over a 10-year period, the use of WMRs has transformed graduate recruitment. Most of the organisations represented here are medium and large employers – those with established graduate training programmes. Smaller firms may be less likely to use all of the techniques noted above, although even here the internet is gradually revolutionising HR practices – in particular, reducing the use of paper-based applications.

Table 25: Weapons of mass rejection (1999–2009)

ASSESSMENT METHOD	1999	2009
Only accept on-line applications	2%	81%
Only accept paper applications	98%	11%
Willing to accept CV	50%	7%
Telephone screening	10%	40%
On-line exercises	2%	36%
Psychometric tests	27%	66%
Personality tests	35%	64%
Numeracy tests	25%	80%
Verbal reasoning	23%	71%
Interviews	100%	98%
Assessment centres	21%	85%

As you can see, in 1999 approximately half of all graduate recruiters were willing to accept CVs. A decade on, this figure had fallen to just 7%, while the proportion of recruiters who will only accept on-line applications had grown from just 2% in 1999 to 81% in 2009. As we will see in Chapter 11, on-line application forms are great news for recruiters, but full of booby-traps for you. And don't expect them to be 'read' by a person; many on-line forms contain electronic data which allow the form to be scanned by computers. If you fail to score enough points you will be rejected ('E-rejected') – sometimes within an hour of submitting the application.

The death knell of the CV

On-line applications have sounded the death knell for the CV – once the cornerstone of the graduate career search. CVs, as far as most graduate recruiters are now concerned, are an anachronism – a Sony Walkman in a world of iPods. Some employers might still accept them; but only to 'flesh out' a candidate's application data. What matters today is how you fare in your on-line application.

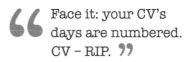
Face it: your CV's days are numbered. CV – RIP.

This might come as a shock. Most people take it for granted that the first task they need to attend to when thinking about their career is write a CV. As a result, you can spend hours drafting and redrafting your curriculum vitae. Some people even pay private consultants to write them on their behalf (never a good idea). The fact is, for most graduate jobs you would be better advised to spend your time gaining relevant work experience, writing better application forms or reading up on how to improve your psychometric test scores.

It's not only on-line application forms which have become more popular with recruiters. The use of telephone screening (or telephone-based interviewing) has grown fourfold in the past decade, and this growth shows no sign of abating. Usually it involves an employer (or an employer's representative) telephoning a candidate and asking them a series of pre-planned questions. The candidate's answers are recorded and given a grade. Failure to score highly enough generally results in rejection from the recruitment process. (In Chapter 12 we will look at how you can boost your chances of passing telephone interviews.)

But it's not on-line applications that students worry about; it's the growing use of tests and psychometric assessments, which now seem to form part of most graduate employers' recruitment processes. Table 25 illustrates just how prevalent these tests have become. So prevalent, in fact, that it's almost inevitable that you will encounter at least some form of such tests when you come to apply for jobs.

Perhaps even more worrying is that, nationally, around half of all graduates fail some form of psychometric test (for some tests, the failure rate is significantly high). But the good news is that practice can make a difference to your scores (see Chapter 13 for how to improve your psychometric test scores).

The final stage in the graduate recruitment process is the assessment centre. Assessment centres can last anything between half a day and two days. Many take place in company premises or specially hired venues. The format of the assessment centre – and how you can improve your performance in them – will be discussed in Chapter 13.

A new dialogue between students and recruiters

What the information in Table 25 makes clear is that psychometric tests and WMRs are not only changing how organisations recruit, they are also rewriting the dialogue between students and recruiters. Behind this are two factors. First: the growing impact of the internet, which is rapidly making paper-based applications redundant. Second: the pressure that graduate recruiters are under to reduce costs and at the same time to ensure that their recruitment is cost-effective.

One of the outcomes of this is that the 'dialogue' between students and recruiters is starting to change. Traditionally, employers used their graduate recruitment process not only as a way of filling their vacancies but also as an opportunity to promote their company brand. To do this, recruiters would try to engage with as many students as possible; they attended dozens of careers fairs, spoke at numerous campus presentations and held literally hundreds of first interviews and assessment centres. For several years, one US consultancy firm used to fly students business-class to New York for second interviews. Even though the firm offered fewer than 1 in 50 a job, its rationale was that after that experience the student would speak highly of the firm for the rest of his or her career. All in all, an expensive way to have people speak well of you!

> The graduate job market was once like *Britain's Got Talent'* – thousands of applicants, some good, some not so good, heats taking place up and down the country. Today, think of *The Apprentice* – fewer, but better prepared competitors, each one having to undertake a series of psychologically designed challenges.

The downside of this approach was not only that it was highly expensive – it wasn't even particularly effective at ensuring that the most suitable graduates were hired.

This is changing. The internet has enabled recruiters both to reduce their costs and to use a more scientific approach to ensuring that the best candidates don't get away. As the graduate recruitment officer for a multinational professional services firm said:

> ❝ Before the credit crunch, we used to use different recruitment methods to help us take candidates through to the assessment centre stage. Now it's the opposite. Our aim this year is to fail more students at a much earlier stage. This will allow us to reduce the money we spend on assessment centres, while also making sure that we get better quality hires. ❞
>
> Graduate recruitment officer, professional services employer

Four essential tactics

The next two chapters introduce you to four essential tactics that will help you prepare for the challenge of applying for graduate jobs. These tactics will help you to write effective applications and CVs; they will give you an insight into how interviews work – while also giving you an inside glimpse of the 25 most predictable questions asked at interviews; they will show you how Assessment Centres work; and, lastly, they will help you to boost your performance in psychometric tests.

The really hard work will have to be done by you; but if practised carefully, these tactics can help to give you the edge over your competitors.

Remember, applying for graduate jobs is very similar to finding yourself a competitor on a TV talent programme (the choice is yours). Most of those who enter the competition are rejected in the first rounds – in fact, the competition is specially designed so that the majority fail in the preliminary stage. Although some of those who go out at this stage are woefully bad, many are simply badly prepared.

The same applies to the graduate job market.

Chapter 10

Applications and CVs

If your application or CV is going to transport you to the higher ground of a job interview, it will need something to help it stand out from the crowd – a Unique Selling Point.

All about USPs

In the last chapter we saw just how many graduate recruiters are turning away from CVs, preferring instead to recruit via on-line application forms. But for some organisations – particularly those without large recruitment programmes – the CV lives on. Just. This chapter looks at the essential information you need to know when writing this most personal and idiosyncratic of all applications.

> " Avoid employing unlucky people – throw half of the pile of CVs in the bin without reading them. "
> David Brent

Stop right there! Don't move a muscle! Before you even begin to write a CV or an application form, ask yourself this:

'What's my USP?'

Unless you know what your USP is (or even *what* a USP is) don't even THINK of writing a CV or an application form. To do so would be to commit the most common error associated with CVs and applications.

So stop what you're doing, and read on.

There are three things that you need to know about CVs:

1. Their life expectancy is very short. In fact, the majority of them are rejected within minutes of landing on a recruiter's desk.
2. Despite the availability of on-line CV templates, most people's CVs make for dreadful reading. Trust me. Some are so bad that they actually wreck any hope the applicant might have had of making it to an interview (see Table 26).

3. Despite what Latinists might tell you, in today's job market, 'curriculum vitae' no longer means writing down everything you can about your life.

Table 26: Ten ways that a bad CV can damage your employability

1.	No Unique Selling Point (USP)
2.	Failing to tell a convincing story (with you as the 'hero')
3.	No relevance to reader/recruiter
4.	Focusing on 'features', not 'benefits'
5.	Factual errors
6.	Inappropriate 'tone of voice'
7.	Spelling mistakes
8.	Poor grammar
9.	Too long
10.	Exaggerating, or making questionable claims

CVs today are sales documents: a pitch to win you a place at an interview. Once you get to an interview, the CV's job is done. No matter how gripping your life story might seem to you, few employers actually want to read the story of your life – not unless it is directly relevant to their bottom line. Instead, they want to discover how you are going to help them solve their business problems. And you have two sides of A4 in which to do it.

This is the reason why most CVs and applications are rejected within minutes of landing on an employer's desk or appearing in their email in-box. They have to be; there simply isn't enough time available for employers to read every application they receive. As a result, they convince themselves that they are highly skilled speed-readers, able to read your CV in less than two minutes.

Two minutes to précis your life, qualifications, work experience and skills.

After this, your CV will be either deleted (shredded, if on paper) or moved to the next stage in the selection process. Attrition rates among CVs and applications are worse than the chances of an overweight salmon trying to swim up a waterfall to its spawning ground: most simply don't make it. In fact, nine out of 10 will be rejected at the first sift.

If your application or CV is going to transport you to the higher ground (eg a job interview) it will need something to help it stand out from the crowd – a USP.

USP is a marketing term and it stands for **UNIQUE SELLING POINT**.

A USP is what makes one product or service stand out from another; it's the difference between good services and excellent services. The concept of a USP is used widely in advertising and is based on three stages:

1. Each advertisement must make a distinct proposition to the consumer
2. This proposition must be one that makes competitors unique – or presented in a unique and distinctive way
3. The USP must be so powerful that it encourages people to want to find out more

Examples of products and services with a strong USP include:

PRODUCT/SERVICE	USP
Head and Shoulders shampoo	'Cures dandruff'
Olay	'You get younger-looking skin'
Domino's Pizza	'Pizza delivered to your door in 30 minutes or your money back'
Rolls Royce	'Luxury and tradition'
Innocent Smoothie	'Healthy, ethical, fun'
Avis car hire	'We try harder – you have to when you're No. 2 in the business'

If your CV or application is going to survive the shredder or dodge the delete button it must have a USP. So what's *your* USP?

How to identify your USP

What constitutes a USP will to some extent depend on which job you're applying for, or which organisation. Your USP demonstrates to the reader – quickly and effectively – how you meet his or her requirements for the post. Your USP could therefore be a skill (team work, proven problem solver, foreign language speaker), an experience (a job in a particularly relevant industry or section – perhaps even an internship in that organisation) or an achievement which marks you out as special. If you are like most students, your greatest achievements to date will probably be those attained in education – qualifications, prizes, school/college-based experiences. Used sparingly, these can be effective in contributing to your USP, but remember to constantly ask yourself how your academic qualifications mark you out as different from the competition.

> " Everyone has a chance to stand out. Everyone has a chance to learn, improve, build up their skills. Everyone has a chance to be a brand worthy of remark. "
> Tom Peters, *The Brand Called You*

Writing your CV

Once you have identified your USP, you can begin thinking about writing your CV and how you want to lay it out. The first and most essential points relate to the length and overall appearance of your CV, and the positioning of your USP within the document.

> " Your CV is your advertisement for you. How it looks and reads is up to you. "

- Two sides of A4 are generally viewed as the maximum length for most UK graduate CVs. American 'resumes' are often shorter – one side of A4.

- If you are going to send a printed copy of your CV, try to use reasonable quality white paper (ie not photocopy paper).

- Think about the positioning of your USP. CV readers generally focus most of their attention on the information on the top half of the first page. Their attention tends to dip by the time they get to the lower half of the second page. For this reason, always make sure that the information you put on the top half of the first page is the most valuable information you want to convey. In other words, the most valuable space on the document is where your USP should be located.

- **What's your lead story?** If your CV is to grab and hold your reader's attention, like a newspaper, it needs a lead story – a key point that grabs them and prompts them to read on. Without a lead story you simply make it easier for the reader to dismiss the CV.

- **Think carefully about the font** – and what it says about you. Times New Roman (safe bet, traditional, little dull)? Arial (business-like but can be informal)? Speaking generally, avoid cranky, informal fonts.

- **Decide how personal you want to be.** Instead of writing from the first-person perspective (eg 'I am a recent graduate ...'), try the third person. This can make your CV flow better; it also avoids every third or fourth word being 'I'.

- **Reverse chronology.** Instead of presenting your information historically (first things first), work backwards, presenting your most recent achievements first and the most distant last. The amount of space that

that information occupies on your CV suggests to the reader the amount of importance you attach to it – so be sure to spend more space on your most recent and relevant attainments, and less space on earlier ones. That way, you avoid giving lots of irrelevant information about events which no longer have a bearing on your career plans.

- **The rounded you.** Recruiters want to hire people who are going to fit into their organisations, who are going to work well in teams and make a contribution socially. Extracurricular achievements are useful in this respect – Duke of Edinburgh Awards, playing for sports teams, representing your university, leading clubs and societies. But writing about such activities always comes with a caution. Always ask yourself what the benefit is of revealing this information to a potential employer. Think about what it might say about you and what impression you want your reader to have of you. Your CV is your advertisement for you – it's your decision what to put in and what to leave out.

- **Establish the right tone of voice.** All CVs have a tone of voice. To the reader, some 'sound' meek and apologetic, others rampantly egotistical. It's all about the words you choose – and how you use them. Although tempting, it's usually best to avoid overselling yourself. After all, eventually, you are going to have to sit in front of your reader and explain just why your 'world class' IT skills are so good; or why, exactly, in your opinion, you are a 'superb candidate' for their firm. A bit of modesty always goes a long way, even if it is false. At the same time, don't undersell yourself. Never use words such as 'it was only' or 'just a holiday job'. Work on the tone of voice, and your CV will never undersell you – nor cause you waves of embarrassment.

- **Proof-read it.** Spelling mistakes are easy to make – and potentially disastrous on a CV, for the simple reason that recruiters expect you to have proof-read your CV dozens of times. Tip: don't trust your own powers of proof-reading – ask a friend or relative to do it for you. Offer them £5 for every error they spot.

- **Qualifications.** For most graduates, a dilemma inevitably arises over which qualifications to include and which to leave out – especially if you have numerous GCSE (or equivalent) qualifications. Again, the best way to approach this is to put yourself in the employer's position. If you are a graduate, your most marketable quali-fication is likely to be your degree, so allocate more space to writing about your degree subject (eg relevant

> WARNING: DELAYS AHEAD!
> 66 Eight out of 10 employers take between one and four months to process job applications. Seven per cent take even longer. 99

modules, dissertations, experiences etc) and consider summarising your GCSEs thus: '*10 GCSEs (grades A–C) including English, Mathematics and Science*'. There is no rule that you must include A Levels or any other grades on your CV; if your grades are less than sparkling, consider, for example: '*A level passes in French, Sociology and Art*'.

Effective applications

Most applications that you make for graduate jobs will be via employers' on-line application forms. As a prime weapon of mass rejection (WMR, see Chapter 10) these are becoming longer and more complicated. The advice in this section aims to help you to give yourself the best chance of getting through to the next round of the application process.

The importance of writing skills

At one time employers struggled to recruit staff with IT and foreign language skills. Now the problem is a shortage of writing skills.

It is generally assumed that if you are able to get into university you will be able to write and spell competently. Many graduate recruiters, however, would disagree that this is the case. In a recent survey by the Association of Graduate Recruiters, six out of 10 recruitment managers claimed that they expected a future shortfall of graduates with 'writing skills'. In some organisations the problem was already so acute that bosses were sending their new graduates trainees on letter-writing courses.

It's vital to avoid spelling and grammar mistakes on your application form. Some employers demand flawless spelling and punctuation; others operate a 'three strikes and you're out' policy, where three spelling mistakes mean your application is automatically rejected. Applicants with dodgy spelling habits will soon find that they can be costly. This year's average starting salary for a graduate job is £24,000. Three spelling mistakes will therefore cost you £1,500 each month in lost earnings. A dictionary will set you back a few pounds.

As in a CV, you need to be sure that you establish the right tone of voice when you are completing application forms. Employers complain that many applications and CVs are too informal and conversational. At all costs, avoid text-speak and other abbreviated forms of writing. They may be popular for communicating with friends, but as far as employers go, text-lingo is definitely not a 'lol' matter. Think of your application as a business document and write it in a business-like and professional tone.

Following instructions, answering questions

Hannah Slaney, Talent Manager at the Cooperative, revealed that last year just one in 10 applications submitted to her organisation were filled in properly. Most were either incomplete or failed to follow basic instructions; some had been copied and pasted from other applications. For Hannah, the problem was that applicants seemed rarely to have taken the time to think about what they wanted to write — and in on-line applications the problem seems to be exacerbated.

If you are going to stand out, your application needs to make a positive impact.

> ❝ Employers recruit candidates who can demonstrate the behaviours which are needed to exceed upon their scheme. Application forms are designed to enable candidates to show that they have the required skills – such as problem solving skills – by answering set questions which probe into specific behaviours. This is why answers such as, '*I do not really have any example for this situation that could be relevant*' are so disappointing. ❞

Hannah Slaney, Talent Manager, Cooperative Group

Poor-quality applications waste everyone's time – the recruiters' and yours. Occasionally, the results can be toe-curling. As Hannah says:

> ❝ Although we encourage candidates to draw upon examples from every part of their lives, some candidates provide information that is inappropriate. For instance, candidates have divulged intimate details regarding parental affairs, arguments with their partners, and their '*ostentatious and party-hard lifestyle*'. Although interesting, the information is surplus to our requirements! ❞

Questions that require applicants to provide examples of their lifetime achievements seem to pose particular problems for many graduates, many still citing their greatest achievement as their degree. While this may be well be the case, it hardly differentiates you from your competitors – not when one in three 18-year-olds now goes into higher education.

Some employers take a range of personal factors into account and are inclined to focus on potential and motivation. Motivation has in fact become a most highly sought after quality with graduate employers. So if you want to impress, make sure that you demonstrate how you have stuck at tasks, maintained your enthusiasm (even in the face of great challenges) and, ultimately, made a difference.

Completing and submitting your application

As we have seen, the graduate job market is a buyers' market. With as many as 80 applicants for every graduate vacancy, it is essential to prepare thoroughly before filling in your application form, and to review it extensively before submitting. Without this, the risks of rejection are great. Your chances of success will rise rapidly when you tailor your application to the organisation to which you are applying. Employers claim that relatively few applicants take the time to do this properly.

One way that you can differentiate yourself from the pack is by stressing the benefits of your work experience. Most employers will invite you to describe incidents and experiences from when you have worked in teams, trained others and implemented new ideas. However, no matter how tempting, try to avoid being too candid.

Treat sections that ask you to disclose your hobbies and personal interests with lots of caution. Research has shown that employers have a pecking order of hobbies and interests which they prefer over others. In general, team sports and competitive challenges are preferred over more solitary pursuits. Employers argue that these sports and hobbies give them an insight into how well you might respond to work-based projects.

- READ EVERYTHING YOU CAN about the job/firm/ employer/industry/profession/sector/field. As a

Before you apply ...

'Competition will be stiff this year and one of the key things that differentiates candidates at application form stage is those who have really done their research. Reading the company website is not enough. Try visiting the business, speak to their people if you can, read reports, look at the competition, search for press articles or coverage as much as possible.'

Rebecca Fielding, Graduate Recruitment Manager, Asda

graduate, you will be expected to be up to date on anything in the news that affects your prospective employer.

- Focus on the recruiters' key requirements as presented in the recruitment literature. Highlight the key skills, qualities, attitudes and experiences that they seek – and make sure that your application emphasises how you meet them.

- Take care to reflect the recruiter's terminology, jargon, vocabulary.

- Be precise with dates and factual information.

- At key points in the application, make sure that you mention the organisation's name (but don't do it too frequently). When done sparingly, this is an effective way to demonstrate your commitment to the organisation.

- Make every word count that you use in your application. Edit out any words that fail to market your USP.

- Because your mind reads what it wants to see, before emailing or posting your application, be sure to have it proof-read.

" We had one graduate apply for a job with us –
their application was excellent and I was about
to recommend that we called the person in for an
interview. Until that was I got to the final question –
"Why do you want to work for this organisation?" In
their answer, the person wrote how they wanted to work
for one of our competitors. It was obvious that they had
copied and pasted their answers from one application to
another – without proof-reading the form. Sadly, I had
no choice but to reject them. "

Graduate recruitment manager, retail

Checklist for writing applications and CVs

1. Make sure that all answers reflect the skills, attitudes and type of person that your prospective employer is in the market to recruit.

2. When filling in application forms, always answer the questions. Avoid the temptation to recycle answers.

3. Have all CVs and application forms carefully proof-read by an expert.

4. Observe the rules – word count, layout, structure.

5. With on-line applications avoid hitting the 'send' button until all the above have been observed.

6. Keep it simple: brief, uncluttered sentences. Avoid jargon. Focus on your key selling points.

7. Never resort to slang or text-speak. Clarify all abbreviations.

8. Show that you have done your homework – use your answers to demonstrate your research.

9. Avoid using passive verbs. Write to attract attention. Ask yourself, 'Is this something I would like to read?'

10. Establish the right tone of voice.

Chapter 11

Interviews

Success or failure at an interview is 80% preparation, 20% delivery.

Preparing for interviews

Despite the many changes occurring in graduate recruitment (as described in Chapter 10), few organisations have yet had the courage to go so far as to abandon the interview. So, whether you love them or loathe them, you're going to have to get used to being interviewed.

> ❝ Death will be a great relief. No more interviews. ❞
>
> Katherine Hepburn

According to theory, the outcome of most interviews is decided within the first two minutes. That means after just 120 seconds the person interviewing you is likely to have made up his or her mind about whether or not to give you the job. A job you could be doing for the next 40 or 50 years of your life.

No wonder that the prospect of an interview inspires such strong feelings of nerves and trepidation. After all, consider how much is at stake. However, despite their fearsome reputation, interviews don't have to be daunting. In fact, with preparation and coaching, you can learn how to transform your interview technique.

There is a growing body of research on job interviews, in particular, on the invisible and subconscious levels at which they operate. What has emerged from these studies is good news for job seekers, for while you should never take it for granted, the days of the Interview from Hell might just be coming to an end.

Interviews – once you take time to understand how they operate – are now far less inscrutable than was first thought. In fact, as this chapter will show you, most interviews are fairly predictable. All of which means that you can prepare for them. Who knows, eventually you might even end up enjoying them!

The focus of this chapter is how to prepare for interviews. By observing the following tips and guidelines given here, there are a number of ways that you can use interviews to your own advantage. To help you prepare, some of the most predictable interview questions asked at interview by real-life employers are listed later in the chapter.

Before the interview

Once you have been offered an interview, the preparation begins. Success or failure at an interview is 80% preparation, 20% delivery. Below are the essential steps you need to take to help you prepare.

What are the selectors looking for?

When recruiting, employers draw up a 'person specification' which lists the ideal skills, knowledge, experience and aptitudes of the successful candidate. Some employers will send you this in the pre-interview pack; others will discuss it in the job description. Either way, *make sure you know what sort of person they are looking to recruit*, and be ready to demonstrate how you meet the criteria.

> " I've missed more than 9,000 shots in my career. I've lost almost 300 games. Twenty-six times, I've been trusted to take the game-winning shot and missed. I've failed over and over and over again in my life. And that is why I succeed. "
>
> Michael Jordan

Make sure you have read the job specification and advert thoroughly. These will give vital clues about what the employer is looking for.

What are you selling?

Identify your key skills, qualities, knowledge and achievements that will set you apart from your competitors. *Always be clear about your USP*. It's this that will get you the job.

Location and length of time

You can tell much about the format of the selection process by checking how long the interview is scheduled to last and where it is to be carried out. If the process is to last more than a couple of hours, you should *expect to face either several interviews or short selection tests.*

Who is interviewing you?

Different people give different styles of interview. Personnel officers tend to focus more on general information: your academic history, what you know about the firm, why you left previous jobs etc. Section heads ask questions more tuned in to their specific section needs. Although this is by no means guaranteed, *knowing who will be interviewing you* can help you with your preparation.

Who is assessing you?

Remember, the likelihood is that you will be assessed by a number of people – not just those asking the questions! In many firms, every person you meet during the day of the interview has an input into the final decision. That means receptionists, secretaries, administrative assistants and even those who you meet 'informally'. Don't fall for the oldest trick in the book: *be prepared!*

What is the format?

Many organisations now use panel interviews when recruiting. That means that you could be faced with a panel of several people, each with their own interests and specialisms (and questions). The number of firms using selection tests and assessments also increases every year; many now ask applicants to provide short presentations or to participate in discussion groups. The idea behind these exercises is the same: to find out what you're really like. *So just be yourself.*

Using STAR to plan your answers

The last thing you want to do when answering questions at an interview is just start talking. Who knows where your answer might lead you, or what you might inadvertently declare. A good way of planning how to answer questions at interviews is to follow the STAR approach.

S: Situation – describe the situation
T: Task or problem – what dilemma or problem did you face?
A: Action – what action did you take?
R: Result – what was the result of your action?

This can be a very effective way of planning your answers. For example, if an interviewer asks you to describe a situation in which you had to overcome a problem, begin by describing the situation – perhaps the event took place during a work placement or during a team project that you were working on as part of your course.

Next, describe the task or problem itself – why was it problematic, what was at stake, how did you recognise that things weren't going as planned?

Then – what action did you take? What did you do that made a difference? Remember, this is your interview, so make sure that you – and your actions – are the main focus of the interview. If the situation you are describing is complex, break your actions up into stages – 'There were three parts to this; first ....'

Finally – and perhaps most crucially of all – you need to help the interviewer to understand the outcomes of your actions and how you evaluated them. This is the part that many graduates get wrong: they forget to say how they measured their success or impact. Because of this, it's never really clear how they know that they solved the problem. As a result, the answer sounds unconvincing.

The STAR approach can be very effective once you have grasped its four stages. It's a good idea always to use it as a basis for answering those interview questions that involve a more detailed answer or ask you to describe the different stages that you went through when solving a problem.

Predictable interview questions

Below is a collection of the 60 or so most predictable questions asked by employers at graduate job interviews. They have been compiled over several years and represent a cross-section of the kinds of questions you can expect to face.

Of course, because every employer is different, every interview will be different, so you are always likely to face questions that don't appear in this list. But at the same time, because recruiters do so many interviews, like everyone, they tend to fall into patterns of established behaviour and to ask similar questions.

It's strongly recommended that before an interview you read through these lists and think about how you might answer the questions. And don't worry: you're unlikely to get all of these questions in one interview!

You may wish to 'take time out' if you find answering some of the questions difficult. Similarly, you may find it easier if you make preliminary notes beforehand.

Work through each section, choosing one or two questions from each. When completed, take a few minutes to reflect on the experience: how did you rate your own performance? Which questions did you find hardest – or easiest – to answer? Why was this so?

Some of these questions might seem fairly straightforward, others less so. A few are tried and tested favourites and as such are almost certain to appear in some shape or form at your next interview. While you don't want to sound over-rehearsed (interviewers seldom appoint robots) it's a useful idea to at least practice answering some of these with a friend. Make it a good friend: someone who's going to challenge you without being overly sympathetic. After all, you want the experience to be as realistic as possible.

Remember: employers don't ask questions at interviews to make you look or feel stupid. Essentially, an interview is just a two-way conversation – the outcome of which will result in you hopefully being offered a job.

And if at the end of the interview you aren't offered the job, don't worry. The law of averages dictates that most people will pass and fail numerous interviews over the course of their careers. So if you don't get the job, dust yourself off, ask for feedback, and work out how your next interview is going to be better.

Warm-up questions

- Tell me about yourself.
- Tell me about your life.
- What should I/we know about you?
- What are your main achievements to date?
- What is in the headlines this morning?
- Where do you want to start?
- Why am I talking to you?
- Why us?
- Why do you want to work for this firm/organisation?
- Why do you want this job?
- Why should we take you on?
- What can you do for us?

- What do you know about this industry?
- What can you contribute to this industry?
- What is your impression of this firm/industry?
- What are the major issues facing us at present?
- Who are our major competitors?
- In your view, where do you think we stand in our industry?
- How could we improve our present standing?
- What is our chairman's/chief executive officer's name?
- What is our share price this morning?
- What is it (what projects are we involved in) that appeals to you?
- Who else have you applied to?
- How did you hear about us?

Academic background questions

- Why did you choose to study those courses?
- Why did you choose to study at that institution?
- Was your college your first choice?
- What relevance has your degree/your qualification got to the real world?
- What extracurricular activities did you become involved in while at college?
- What have you gained from your qualifications?
- Do you think students should be expected to pay for their education?
- What employment-related skills did you pick up while studying?

- What relevance has your degree/your qualification got to our firm/this job?
- What has your degree/qualification really taught you?
- How has your vacation work contributed to your career aspirations?

Questions about you

- What are you looking for in your first/next job?
- How do you see your career developing over the next five years?
- Why do you think you will be a success in the position you are applying for?
- Which newspapers do you read?
- What time management strategies do you use? Do they always work? How do you prioritise?
- What things annoy or upset you? What makes you lose your temper?
- How do you deal with problems? Give some examples.
- How would your best friend (or worst enemy) describe you?
- What is the most difficult thing you have ever had to deal with?
- Which historical figures do you most identify with? Why?
- When have you had to introduce change into your work/life/course? Tell me about it.

Criteria-based questions

- Give an example of when you have contributed to the working of a team. What is your preferred role in a team?
- When have you had to provide a solution to a complex problem? What did you do and were you successful?
- Give an example of when you influenced the work of others. What did you do? How did you achieve it? What were the outcomes?
- When have you been responsible for the actions of others? Give examples. What was your role? How did you overcome any difficulties?

Direct challenges

- What are your weaknesses?
- What are the situations that you find hardest to handle? Give some examples.
- How can you account for your low A level grades/ GCSEs/degree/HND?
- Why did you leave your last job?
- How would you feel working for someone older/ younger than yourself?
- What skills and qualities do you need to improve – and how do you intend to achieve this?
- How geographically mobile are you?
- How much do you expect to be paid?
- If you were me/us, what would you look for in a candidate for this post?
- How soon could you start?

- To make sure we get a good picture of you, what else should we know about you?
- What is your criterion for measuring success?
- If you were the CEO of this organisation, what would you do first?
- Give an example of when you had to deal with difficult people. How did you handle the situation and what strategies did you employ?

Scenario questions

- You are the manager of a large supermarket. It is 5pm on Christmas Eve. The store is full to capacity with shoppers. Suddenly there is a power cut and the store is plunged into darkness. What do you do?
- You are the brand manager for a well-known confectionery firm. One day you are sent a note telling you that some of your brands have been intentionally contaminated with a lethal substance before leaving the warehouse and being dispatched to the retail outlets. What do you do?
- It is the beginning of October, half way through the financial year, and you have found out that you have run out of money. What should you do?
- You have been put in charge of introducing car-parking charges for staff working in the organisation. How would you set about tackling the situation?

And finally

Good interviewers allow a space for candidates to ask the interviewer – or the interviewing panel – some questions. Don't feel that you have to ask questions; if all your questions have been answered during the selection procedure, then say so.

That said, interviews provide excellent good opportunity to obtain clarification on certain points (such as career advancement, training and future responsibilities) and they can also be an excellent opportunity for you to make an impression with senior managers.

The following may give you an idea of the sorts of questions you could ask:

- Where could I be in five years' time within the firm?
- What have previous graduates gone on to achieve within the organisation?
- What are the company's plans for the future?
- What further training can you offer me?
- What are the conditions of service? (If not already specified)
- Is there a staff appraisal system in place? How does it operate?
- How frequently would I meet with my line manager to review my progress?
- What sort of induction programme have you planned for the new post?
- Who would I report to on a daily basis? What is that person's key function?
- When can I expect to hear from you? How will you contact me?

The secret of the perfect interview

Ask employers why they chose one interviewee over another, and they will tell you that the successful candidate possessed the right skills, experience, qualities and motivation for the job. Listen carefully, and most will make the process of recruitment and selection sound highly objective – almost like a scientific experiment. Subjective feelings, emotions, ideas and gut reactions will have had little or no effect on the outcome.

❝ **How you come across is more important than what you say.** ❞

The truth, however, is rarely so straightforward.

A number of academic studies have been published in the last five years which have found that, far from conducting exercises in objectivity, interviewers are often deluding themselves about how they make up their minds and that, in practice, most are subconsciously swayed by forces beyond their own cognition.

For example, one study found that, regardless of their academic qualifications, work experience and skills, candidates who appeared to have pleasant personalities were almost always at a greater advantage than those who met all the above criteria but whose personality seemed less friendly. You might think this should be fairly obvious. Well, not if you are a graduate recruiter who prides herself on her objectivity and lack of bias.

The implications are staggering, for they reveal for the first time the **Number 1 rule** of interviews: *How you come across is more important than what you say.*

Interviews: the personal factor

Successful interview candidates don't just possess the right skills, experience and knowledge. By looking enthusiastic and motivated, they also manage to form a bond with the interviewer. To put it another way, the interviewer finds the person they are interviewing to be both pleasant and 'likeable'. Ultimately, it is this completely subjective and personal factor that makes all the difference when it comes to deciding who is in and who is out.

According to one psychologist, during interviews 'likeability' is more important than academic achievements and work experience. You can have superb qualifications and work experience, but if the person interviewing doesn't feel you are someone with whom they would want to spend time working with, you're unlikely to get the job.

How can you use this knowledge to boost your chances of interview success?

How to shine at interview

- Find something that you genuinely like about the organisation and let your opinion about it be known
- Smile, and tell the interviewer how pleased you are to be offered an interview with that organisation
- Be prepared to give the interviewer a genuine compliment
- If appropriate, be prepared to chat about a non-job-related topic that you and the interviewer find interesting
- Make sure that you show you are interested in the interviewer and the organisation. For example, ask about the type of person they are looking for, and how the job fits into the overall organisational structure
- Be ready to show your enthusiasm about the job and the organisation
- Maintain eye contact with the interviewer. Give a good, positive handshake

Striking the right tone

So far, so good. But what if you have something in your past life that you would rather hadn't occurred? Is there ever an ideal time during an interview in which to bring a skeleton out of the cupboard?

Apparently, there is. Researchers have found that it's usually

> **An air of casual modesty is always preferable to rampant egotism.**

better to disclose weaknesses as early as possible in the interview. That way, you have lots of time left in which to rebuild the interviewers' confidence in you. The likelihood is that this will be completely counter-intuitive to what your instinct tells you to do. Most people, when faced with airing areas of weakness often choose to wait until the end of the interview before letting it slip out that they left a previous job under a cloud, or that their exam grades were less than sparkling. This is the worst approach to take. Psychologists suggest that by mentioning a weakness early on, you can actually give your credibility a boost by getting the weakness into the conversation towards the start of the interview.

With achievements, the exact opposite is true.

Examples of great personal achievements are generally best left until the end of the interview. Why? Because waiting until the interview is drawing to a close before casually disclosing that you have recently climbed Everest, swum the channel, saved the polar bear from extinction, or are about to be named in the Queen's Birthday Honours list is far more impressive than blurting it out as soon as the interview gets under way. An air of casual modesty is always preferable to rampant egotism.

Second chance to make a first impression

So what happens if you make a mistake during the interview? Is it game, set and match, or merely the end of round one?

During interviews, most candidates make mistakes of varying degrees of importance. Few of them are really important; they are more a reflection of the candidate's nerves than of his or her cognitive abilities. Fortunately, most interviewers are fairly forgiving of mistakes made during interviews and are more than willing to make allowances. In fact, one psychologist has found that many employers didn't even notice mistakes and were more than willing to let the candidate restart an answer.

This lets you in to the **Number 2 rule** of interviews: *mistakes that to you may seem to be of a major consequence are rarely as noticeable to interviewers*, so don't get caught up in making excessive apologies. They could actually make things worse by drawing further attention to your mistake.

If you do make a mistake in one of your answers, apologise quickly and ask permission to start again. Smile, and then, as if nothing untoward had happened, take it from the top. The chances are that the interviewer will be impressed with your confidence and self-assurance.

And remember, even interviewers sometimes feel nervous in interviews!

Telephone interviews

There's no denying it: the telephone has become an integral and unavoidable part of our lives. We couldn't do without it. In the not-so-distant-past (ie 10 years ago) owning a car was the ultimate symbol of coming of age. Today, it's receiving your first mobile phone. Top Gear? Top phone, more like.

> 66 The telephone is such an important invention that one day every town will have one. 99
>
> Alexander Graham Bell

The worldwide number of mobile phone users is now estimated at 1.6 billion. The fastest growing area of the market is among young people. A new study by NOP World indicates that 44% of 'teens' and 'tweens', between the ages of 10 and 18, now possess a phone. Mobile phone ownership has increased from 13% to

40% among 12- to 14 year-olds, and from 42% to 75% among 15- to 17-year-olds. Little wonder that recently the *Independent* reported that a group of young people who had agreed to go without their phones for two weeks as an experiment told researchers that their social lives had fallen apart.

Got your lines crossed?

But owning a phone isn't the same as being effective on the phone, and despite the numbers of phones in use, few people have actually taken the time to master telephone skills. As a result, each year countless telephone interviews are failed, business opportunities lost, relationships ruined, friendships ended (to say nothing of the number of wrong pizza toppings ordered) – all through a lack of telephone skills.

Few telephone conversations are as important and potentially life-changing as telephone interviews. This section looks at how, with practice, even experienced telephone users can learn how to improve their skills.

The rise of the telephone interview

Graduate recruiters use telephone interviews for a number of reasons. First, with no way to take in visual signals, they are a very effective means of assessing your communication skills (for this reason, many telephone interviews are recorded).

Second, telephone interviews are a very good way to save money. Face-to-face interviews are expensive and time consuming; phone interviews offer employers a powerful opportunity to cut down on travel expenses. To cut costs even further, many firms now outsource telephone interviews to offshore call centres. This means that the person interviewing you may be speaking from the other side of the world.

But as a weapon of mass rejection (WMR, see Chapter 10), telephone interviews are very good at providing employers with a basis on which to reject applicants. You really can't afford not to take them seriously.

Preparing for telephone interviews

World-class telephone skills begin with preparation. Before picking up the phone, make sure you know what the objective is for the call is – and what you intend the outcome to be. It really is *your* call.

First step: Acquire the right equipment – sharp pencil (pens have a habit of mysteriously running out of ink at crucial moments) and several blank pieces of paper.

When speaking to an employer or recruiter, make sure you

Average time duration of a telephone interview:

60 mins – 7%
40 mins – 7%
35 mins – 7%
30 mins – 36%
25 mins – 14%
20 mins – 29%

Source: University of Kent

know exactly to whom you are speaking, and why. Which department are they in? What is their job title? Furthermore, what exactly is the objective of the interview? Where does it stand in the recruitment process?

Location, location, location!

You have to believe that this is the MOST IMPORTANT CALL YOU WILL EVER MAKE. If you don't, rest assured: it won't be. The location for the call has to be perfect.

Second step: Serve eviction orders on all those who might want to use the same room as you. This order has to be enforceable for the duration of your call. For some reason, dogs and small children are mysteriously drawn to rooms in which potentially life-changing telephone calls are taking place. So make sure that you inform all potential disturbers about what you are doing. Beg, if need be even pay, someone to answer the door for you when – as will happen – the doorbell rings while you are in mid-interview. Muzzle yapping dogs. And warn those who may possibly beat you to a ringing phone that you are expecting a major call.

Establish the facts

In the midst of life-changing phone calls, even the most intelligent minds can go blank. But while Blank Mind Syndrome is pardonable in a three-hour physics exam, it is less excusable when the question is, 'What is your postcode?' You will need to be 100% clear and accurate on the following: your grades, intended study programme, course codes, name and address of your referee, etc.

Third step: Write a mini-CV containing all pertinent information. Keep this next to the phone.

Dress for success

Strange but true: the way you are dressed while taking an important telephone call can play a major role in how you perform (yes, 'perform') on the phone. Those who dress smartly tend to outperform those who don't. Not only do they feel more prepared, they generally feel more confident when addressing recruiters. (The opposite is also true.) Next time you make an important call, try it.

Stand up

There are two reasons why the best telephone calls are when people stand up to make them. First, standing up helps with blood flow and breathing techniques. Second, the added height can provide the caller with an important psychological advantage. Either way, voices tend to sound better when the speaker is standing up. When did you last see Prime Minister's Question Time conducted sitting down?

Script it

Before the telephone interview, spend a few minutes jotting down the key points of what you want to say – the issues you want to raise and the points you want to make. Use bullet points – key words, phrases and outcomes. Write down difficult words – such as the name of the graduate job you're applying for, the department that you hope to work in, even the CEO's name. But always resist the temptation to write a script. Recruiters are rarely impressed by Dalek-like speeches. Your aim is to sound natural, confident, enthusiastic to join their organisations and, of course, pleasant (see earlier in this chapter 'The secret of the perfect interview').

Breathe; slow down; smile

An amazing 70% of the information that we take in while talking to people is visual. In other words, it has little to do with verbal communication. This means that what you say on the telephone – AND HOW YOU SAY IT – assumes larger-than-life importance. Before making the call, take some deep breaths. Speak more slowly and more clearly than you normally would (particularly if you have an accent, or a tendency to speak rapidly). Remember to smile! An old radio trick, but listeners can clearly 'hear' a smiling voice. Not only does smiling put you in a good mood, it also makes the voice sound fresh, enthusiastic, confident and in control.

Beware: telephone virgins

Several years ago, a student telephoned the London head office of Virgin to apply for a part-time job. Sir Richard Branson answered the phone. For a brief moment, the student realised that he had the undivided attention of one of the most influential and powerful people in the country. All he could think of to say was, 'Can I have an application form, please?' The moment had passed, an opportunity had been lost.

> **The most important part of a phone conversation is the introduction – the part said by you before the other person has their say. If their first comment is negative, the chances are that it's downhill all the way. If positive, you're in with a shot.**

The laws of 'telequette'

Your interviewer should introduce him or herself to you and explain briefly how the interview is going to work. Next, they will give you a chance to introduce yourself and say a few words about your achievements. Make your introduction lively, interesting and clear. Don't waffle; when you have said all you need to say to make a good impression, stop, and let them ask you the next question.

Golden rule of telephone interviews

How you come across is as important as what you say. Think about it. Make sure you avoid at all costs, slang, long pauses, poor grammar and saying anything – ANYTHING – risqué or controversial. Never lose your temper or become confrontational. Don't try to be too smart. There really was only one Oscar Wilde.

Manners + Preparation = Success

As phone ownership has increased, telephone manners seem to have declined. This is due partly to the phone's having become an informal item of leisure, a fashion accessory. Thanks to call centres, 'phone rage' is also becoming more common. Never have good telephone manners been more important!

Good manners – on the phone? With no visual images available, listeners 'hear' good manners far more acutely than they would in a face-to-face conversation. Listen to great phone users, and you will hear them being almost obsessively polite when making important calls. Count how many times they use phrases such as 'thank you', 'that's very kind of you', 'if you don't mind', and again, 'thank you'. They do this not because they're creeps, but because long ago they discovered that being polite is an easy way to score big points in difficult phone conversations. If you are feeling tongue tied, it also gives you something SAFE, IMPRESSIVE and POSITIVE to say. Consciously try to 'big up' your phone voice. Be slightly larger than life – interested, enthusiastic, sounding like you're having fun. After all, you *do* want that place!

All this is equally important for how you *answer* the phone. Remember: recruiters occasionally contact applicants direct, without giving them prior notice. This means that you will need to be prepared at all times to go into recruitment mode. Let's face it – this is one phone call you don't want your two-year-old sister, or 90-year-old grandmother to pick up first.

Commit nothing to memory – not even your address

Write down all key information: names, addresses, and telephone numbers. Email addresses in particular – theirs and yours. Ask the other person to spell any unusual or difficult names. Commit nothing to memory. Check that you have things written down correctly. Before putting the phone down, you must be 100% confident that you know exactly what will happen next. This is your big chance. Make it count.

Think it's all over? It is now

Don't waffle, no matter how well you feel the phone call is going. Aim to impart all relevant information, but avoid being too candid; this is a 'sales' situation, after all. The danger of waffling is that you can easily stray into uncharted territory, saying something that, on reflection, might have been better left unsaid (another reason why sticking closely to the script is so important). Check, check and check again that you've obtained all the information that you need. If necessary, ask if you can check with them that you have understood things correctly (another useful technique for demonstrating self-confidence and maturity). If you have made the call, you should be the person who ends the conversation. If not, leave it to the other person. Before the call ends, make sure (again) that you have the person's name and number. Ask for their direct line (if you don't already have it).

Afterwards, if possible, enter the details into your computer. That way, the information can't be lost, tucked behind a sofa, washed in the washing machine or eaten by a toddler.

Make that call – now!

Telephone calls should never be postponed. If you are nervous about making the call today, you will be twice as nervous about making it tomorrow. Do it now, and then learn from your mistakes. And remember to try to enjoy the experience. The employer's job is to recruit graduates – they want to hire you.

Chapter 12

Assessment centres and tests

Think of the assessment centre as a bit like being on *The Apprentice* – instead of trying to assess your suitability for the job in one interview, employers use the assessment centre as an opportunity to look at you over an extended period.

Assessment centres

Assessment centres have been around since the First World War, when the German army introduced them as a means of selecting officers. Since then, they have been used by many medium-sized and large organisations to recruit and select graduates. Lasting for between half a day and two full days, assessment centres are often the final obstacle between you and your dream job. So what do they consist of, and how can you give yourself the best possible chance of passing them?

Your invitation to an assessment centre usually comes after you have passed a first interview with a graduate recruiter. Assessment centres can take place either on the employer's premises or at a specially hired venue.

Because they take place over an extended period of time and bring you into contact with a number of representatives from the organisation, employers generally see assessment centres as offering the fairest and the most 'objective' way of recruiting

> At the assessment centre, we're looking to see how people interact, how they behave in different situations and contexts.
>
> Graduate recruitment manager, investment banking

graduates. Think of the assessment centre as a bit like being on *The Apprentice* – instead of trying to assess your suitability for the job in one interview, employers use the assessment centre as an opportunity to look at you over an extended period.

Assessment centres generally involve a number of stages, which are described below.

Social and informal introductions

Assessment centres generally begin with an introductory stage, where you are introduced to the other candidates, the assessors and other members of staff from the organisation. If this sounds relatively informal, it isn't. Although this stage is often presented to candidates as the ideal opportunity for them to find out about the organisation and to ask questions in a more casual setting, in reality they are being observed and assessed right from the start. Avoid being 'off your guard'; similarly, make sure that you appear enthusiastic and motivated. After all, you want the job! If there is a bar available, avoid excessive consumption. And remember, every member of staff that you meet from the employer's organisation is likely to have a say in the final assessment. That includes receptionists, porters, senior managers and even past graduates whom you meet at dinner.

Information sessions

Typically, these tend to be lectures or presentations about various aspects of the job or organisation. You should approach them as opportunities to learn more about your prospective employer; and, through one or two well-chosen questions, as a chance to demonstrate your enthusiasm and commitment. Make sure that you listen carefully to everything you are told. If you're not clear about something, ask. But make sure your questions aren't duff ones: inappropriate questions can damage the overall impression that you make.

Group discussions and presentations

Most assessment centres include group discussion exercises where you and the other candidates are asked to discuss a topic or issue. Usually, these discussions will be observed by assessors. Occasionally, 'roles' will be allotted to each group member — chairperson, time-keeper, etc. If, however, you are in a group in which no roles have been allocated, it's always a good idea, before the discussion begins, to clarify the amount of time available and to ask other group members if roles should be agreed. You don't necessarily have to appoint yourself to a particular role, but offering to be the time-keeper can score you easy points with the assessors, while also ensuring that your group keeps to the task in hand.

During the discussion, don't feel that you have to dominate the conversation – you do, however, need to make sure that your opinions are heard. Making sure that the discussion sticks to the subject in question can be another way of scoring relatively easy points – as can ensuring that every member of the group has a chance to voice their opinions. Make sure that you constantly monitor your body language – even if your attention begins to wander, be sure to look enthusiastic and engaged with the task. Smile, and maintain eye contact.

> ❝ During the group discussion, everyone was talking like mad and I found it really hard to join in. The only thing I said was, 'I think we've gone off the point'. Later, one of the assessors told me they had been impressed by this because it showed confidence and analytical skills. ❞
>
> Graduate management trainee

Tests and exercises

Most assessment centres involve different types of tests designed to reveal your cognitive skills and behavioural characteristics. Some of these tests (ie cognitive) are used by assessors to record literacy, numeracy and analytical skills. Behavioural tests tend to record different aspects of your personality. Some of these tests are notoriously difficult and have been designed so that, within the time available, few people will ever finish them. Don't worry if you think you have fared badly in these tests; most assessment centres are based on how you perform across all of the exercises involved.

Formal dinner

Graduate recruiters want to hire you not only because of your academic skills but because of your all-round personality. After all, that's what will help you to build strong networks with clients. For this reason, most assessment centres will have a formal dinner towards the end of the time. These can be daunting occasions, but remember: the aim of formal dinners is twofold. First, to give the assessors another (final) chance to observe you in a business setting; and second, to give you an insight into what it's really like to work for that organisation. As such, you'll meet lots of people from the organisation, including recently hired graduates – people who, a year earlier, were in the same position as you. They can offer you a mine of useful information.

Final interview

Most assessment centres conclude with a final interview. This is usually a panel interview in which you will be assessed by several managers. This is often also the final stage of the entire selection process. After this, you will face one of two possible outcomes: you will either be offered the job or turned down.

Assessment centres – 10 top tips

1. Take it as read that everything you do during an assessment centre is being – well – assessed. Be yourself, by all means, but don't forget this essential point.

2. Everyone you meet from the employer's organisation is likely to be assessing you and will contribute to the final decision whether or not to hire you. That includes receptionists, administrative staff, porters and the new graduate trainees whom you sat next to during dinner.

3. There is no such thing as 'off the record' at assessment centres, so never let your guard down – even during the 'informal' events such as dinners and social evenings.

4. Remember: at assessment centres, how you come across is as important as what you say, so make sure that you join in every exercise (even if you think the task is stupid), be sure to sound enthusiastic, always be ready with a question, and support others.

5. If you are set a group task, score easy points by volunteering to be the time-keeper, note-taker or chairperson. If a member of your group seems withdrawn or hasn't had his or her opinions taken into consideration, be the one who makes sure that everyone has a chance to contribute.

6. In discussions you don't need to be the one who says the most – but you do need to make sure that you get your opinions and ideas across. Employers want to recruit graduates who are analytical but also practical; showing how you have come to a decision always goes down well – particularly if your decision has been arrived at after consulting with others.

7. Behaviour is everything. Employers want to see that you are 'likeable' and a good team player. Smile, show that you have a sense of humour and never, in any circumstance, lose your composure. Avoid free bars.

8. In group discussions, don't be dogmatic – no matter how provoked you are. Being ready to change your mind, if appropriate, can demonstrate that you are pragmatic and likely to fit in with others. But if you don't agree with the consensus, say so! Standing your ground is an essential management trait.

9. Before the assessment centre, prepare one or two 'interesting' issues about which you could talk. Assessment centres often require you to give a brief presentation on a subject of your choice. Having a prepared subject up your sleeve will make a big

difference. Don't make it too technical or complicated –remember, you'll probably be presenting to a cross-disciplinary team.

10. Don't play mind games with other candidates. No matter how much it feels as if you are contestants on a reality TV programme, you're competing not with each other but against an objective standard. Be yourself, be interesting and, most of all, be prepared.

Psychometric tests

As we saw in Chapter 10, more than 70% of recruiters use some type of psychometric test or assessment when hiring graduates. This means that no matter what job or sector you are planning to enter, you have a better than even chance of encountering one of them. So what are they, and what do they measure?

Because most recruiters' tests are based on measuring your psychological make-up, the common name for them is 'psychometric tests'. In recent years, these have become very popular. When recruiting graduates, employers use roughly two forms of tests.

Computer says no

The first are cognitive tests, designed to measure your intellectual capacity. These tests are usually against the clock and are taken under exam-like conditions. Employers who use these tests are particularly keen to measure your intellectual capacity for thinking and reasoning, especially your logical or analytical skills.

Traditionally, these tests were only encountered towards the end of the assessment. Today, however, you can experience them on-line as part of the first stage of the application process. Failure to score a sufficiently high grade can lead to automatic rejection (it has been claimed that half of all graduates fail cognitive assessments).

Most of these first-stage tests are designed for a generic graduate job – so you're unlikely to be tested on specific job roles. In most tests, accuracy is more important than speed (few candidates complete all the questions in these tests). On the whole, the tests tend to be based on multiple-choice questions. It is sometimes possible to obtain a list of sample questions from the employer prior to taking the test.

Personality inventories

Personality inventories are designed to assess your personality characteristics, and attempt to predict how you might react or behave in various work-related situations. Unlike ability or aptitude tests, personality inventories are rarely timed and typically there are neither 'right' nor 'wrong' answers to choose from. The idea is to be consistent with your own values and principles and to answer accordingly. The reason why employers use personality inventories is to find out whether you will fit in with their organisational culture. They also want to see how your personality might affect your style of team work. Because every team is different, practising these tests is unlikely to give you an advantage when applying for jobs. What it will do, however, is help you to gain a useful insight into your personality preferences (an insight which can help you with your choice of career). But practising these tests is unlikely to make you a better candidate. One good thing about personality inventories is that you can neither pass nor fail them. All you can do is be yourself.

How your university careers service can help

To find out more about psychometric tests and assessments, your university careers service will be able to point you to a range of in-house resources, all of which have been put together to give you an insight into how they operate.

The Association of Graduate Careers Advisory Services (AGCAS) has a battery of tests that it runs in conjunction with Saville & Holdsworth – one of the world's leading testing centres. Many of these tests are used by graduate recruiters, so familiarising yourself with them will give you a useful head start.

The tests available measure your verbal, numerical and diagrammatical reasoning skills and can be accessed both on-line and via careers service seminars. Ask at your careers service for more details.

The most commonly used personality inventory is currently the Myers Briggs Type Indicator (MBTI). Based on the psychology of Carl Jung, MBTI measures your personal preferences and can help to assess, among other indicators, whether you are an extrovert or an introvert, and whether you prefer a judging or a perceiving approach to the outer world. Again, your careers service will be able to advise you how to find out more about MBTI and other personality inventories.

On-line resources

Although it's not possible to pass or fail a personality inventory, ability tests are a different matter entirely. One survey found that 50% of graduates fail numeracy and literacy tests. This means that the more practice you have working on these tests, the better.

You can practise psychometric tests on-line, here are a few websites to try:

- ASE-Solutions
  www.ase-solutions.co.uk/support.asp?id=62
- Psychological Testing Centre (British Psychological Society)
  www.psychtesting.org.uk/
- Saville & Holdsworth (SHL Direct)
  www.shldirect.com/

E = Employability,
Q = Qualifications,
WE = Work Experience,
S = Strategies and
C = Contacts

$$E = Q + WE + S \times \textbf{C}$$

"The only really valuable thing is intuition."

Albert Einstein

Chapter 13

The final component of the formula

When more people than ever have qualifications, work experience and skills, having contacts assumes ever greater importance.

Demonstrating commitment and motivation

As the competition for graduate jobs intensifies, demonstrating to employers how you stand out from other graduates is becoming increasingly difficult. As we have already seen, today's graduate job market is dominated by an oversupply of students from similar educational backgrounds, each one offering a cocktail of similar qualifications, similar grades and even similar types of work experience.

For you and other students, this presents a problem. As far as other generations were concerned, the greatest challenge was keeping up with the in-crowd. Today, it's how to stand out from the in-crowd, how to demonstrate your uniqueness.

The surplus society presents employers with a problem as well. Faced with thousands of nearly identical applications, they are switching their recruitment and selection methods to ensure that they hire only those who can demonstrate extra commitment and motivation – old-fashioned qualities that haven't been much heard of in recent years. But how do you demonstrate commitment and motivation?

Answering this question forms the basis of the final section.

Knowing me, knowing you

Since the economic downturn, the value of contacts in the formula for graduate employability has been rising steadily. When more people than ever have qualifications, work experience and skills, having contacts assumes ever greater importance. Nevertheless, just how quickly the value of contacts has risen has taken most people by surprise.

For example, to help students gain contacts with graduate recruiters, recruitment organisations are now selling internships on the open market. According to the national press, internships in highly popular job sectors such as the media are even selling for as much as £8,000. The willingness of some people to pay large amounts of money for the privilege of working in an organisation for as little as three or four weeks has little to

> **It's not *what* you know, it's not *who* you know. It's *who* knows you.**

do with the traditional reason why people undertake work experience, ie to acquire certain skills or gain an insight into a particular occupational sector. It's because internships (as we saw in Chapter 9) are a fantastic way of gaining contacts. And contacts – as everyone who's in a job will tell you – lead to jobs.

The role that contacts play in making you employable has tended to be underemphasised by careers experts. This is partly because acknowledging that employability might also depend on something in addition to qualifications, skills and experience is potentially problematic. After all, when it comes to contacts and networks, some people will always be better positioned than others to take advantage.

But this is to miss an important point: with practice and coaching, everyone can develop and enhance their personal contacts and networks. You might never get to the stage where you have President Obama or Sir Richard Branson on speed-dial but, with time, perseverance and a plan, you will be amazed at how quickly and effectively your network starts to grow. So what is networking – and why are contacts so important?

The original social networking

'Networking' is a term used to describe a process whereby you make it your business to get to know people – people whose shared expertise, knowledge, enthusiasm, experience, ideas and contacts will take you a step closer to your chosen career.

Networking succeeds because, of all the job-seeking strategies, this is the one that most closely approximates to normal human behaviour. Think of it like this: let's say you want to go to Morocco for your summer holidays but are unsure about the best places to stay. A friend knows of someone who recently went there and has lots of books and magazines on the country. Your friend offers to invite the would-be expert over to meet you, so that the two of you can discuss your travel arrangements. Your friend contacts this person on your behalf and they turn out to be only too glad to come and talk with you – after all, there's nothing they like better than to reminisce about their holiday in Marrakesh.

> 66 We all need a strong support network. Even though I was taught to stand on my own feet, without my loyal family and friends I would be lost. 99
>
> Sir Richard Branson, *Screw it, let's do it, Lessons in life* (2006)

This, essentially, is how networking works – it's about people with shared interests coming together to swap ideas and experiences, with the sole objective of getting things done.

What networking isn't taking advantage of others, cutting corners, excluding people, all but the privileged few; or a by-word for not having to play by the rules. None of this is networking; it's cheating.

Networking has always existed and always occurred – in fact, it far outdates any of our modern job-seeking strategies. This is because it operates purely and simply through human interaction. It's about establishing a set of contacts among people with common social, professional or career interests. Its goal is to provide you with an opportunity to gain information from people who have a particular insight into or expertise in a particular career field. These people don't have to be industry leaders; they don't even need to be in management posts. What they do need to have is a particular insight or experience, or contact with an industry or job in which you are interested.

The key to networking

The key to building a good network is to know why you need it. Having a clear objective is the best way to start networking. Your objective could be to help you find a job in a particular sector; similarly, it could be to learn more about a particular career. Either way, before you begin talking to people, you need to take time to establish what it is that you want to gain from the interactions. Once you're clear about your networking objectives, your conversations will have a greater purpose and sense of direction. From this, you will gain more contacts.

In networking, the more you give, the more you gain. World-class networkers never begin conversations by asking themselves what they can gain from the interaction. Their approach is quite different. They ask what information they can *provide* to the contact – how they can help the contact with his or her business problem, and what introductions they can make for him or her. Selfless and altruistic? Hardly! Great networkers know that the more they can help their contacts, the more help will come their own way. This is because people love to help those who have helped them. Consider, for example, the curious case of Benjamin Franklin.

The Franklin Syndrome

Benjamin Franklin, the 18th-century politician, writer, scientist and thinker wrote that '*He that has once done you a kindness will be more ready to do you another than he whom you yourself have obliged.'* In other words, if a person does you a favour – such as introducing you to someone who can help you with a job application – that person will be more inclined to help you again in the future. In fact, they will be more willing to help you than someone whom you yourself have helped. This theory, known as the Franklin Syndrome, goes to the heart of networking and tells you all you

> **He that has once done you a kindness will be more ready to do you another than he whom you yourself have obliged.** "
>
> Benjamin Franklin

need to know about why networking is the ultimate job search strategy. The more that people do for you, the more they want to continue.

Well, up to a point. Of course, everyone has their limits. No one wants to feel exploited or used. To be effective, networking has to be based on strong values and complete honesty; you need to be rigorous and ultra principled. People will only network with you if they feel (note: *feel*, not *think*) that they are being respected and that you are not using them as a means of cheating the system.

How to build a network

The great thing about networking is that there is always a very good chance that the contacts you need to get you started are just a handshake away. In other words, you almost certainly know someone right here, right now, who can introduce you to that first person who will form the basis of your network. That person could be a fellow student, a tutor, a careers adviser or a family member. Whoever they are, they are probably within touching distance.

That's another considerable advantage of networking – you can network anywhere, making new and interesting contacts as you go along. Once you acquire the networking mindset, you can take advantage of almost any opportunity to start building your network.

For most networkers, the most common places to network are conferences, professional events and exhibitions. Attending careers fairs, departmental seminars and business events, such as those run for students by local chambers of commerce can be particularly good, enabling you to meet contacts in your local area.

The importance of a business card

Before you start networking, you will need your own business card. Despite the rising competition for jobs, few students and graduates have their own business cards – a lost opportunity with serious consequences. Go to any careers fair, and you will see students and graduates jotting their names and addresses

> 66 Emails are deleted, CVs are shredded, addresses are lost, but business cards are always retained. 99

on scrappy pieces of paper before handing them over to employers. A business card would set you aside as different, professional and prepared – three essential employability qualities.

You may think a business card is old fashioned, but the fact is no one ever – EVER! – throws them away. This means that business cards are an excellent and relatively cheap way of making sure that a contact never forgets your name. Emails are deleted, CVs are shredded, addresses are lost, but business cards are always retained.

Not that your business card has to be elaborate or expensively designed. Forget trendy designs. All you need, at this stage, is a plain piece of card with your name, address, email name and phone number. Then get lots of copies made. Once your network starts to grow, you'll need them!

Business cards have another strategic advantage. If you give someone your card it's very difficult for them, socially, to avoid returning the favour. As a result, you'll soon find that the more cards you hand out, the more you receive. Automatically, your network will start to grow. All because of a 3 x 2 inch piece of white card!

Recording contacts

Because networking can happen anywhere, it is essential that you get into the habit of recording your contacts. At the very least, you need to find a way to record your contacts' details. There are numerous ways you can do this; but what matters is that their details are easily accessible, wherever you are.

A contacts database can be particularly effective, even if it's just a folder containing all the business cards you've managed to collect. Keep notes on when and where you met the contact and what was discussed. You never know when a contact may come in handy!

Information interviewing

How do you get to speak to people with whom you share no mutual contacts? The answer lies in an American job-search technique known as 'information interviewing', and it's one of the most powerful and effective career management tools.

> The aim of information interviewing is simple: to help you learn more about a job or organisation.

The term 'information interviewing' is used to describe the process whereby, instead of waiting for jobs and leads to appear in newspapers or on-line job sites, you take your destiny into your own hands and instigate short meetings with key personnel who are currently employed in organisations or occupations in which you are interested.

The aim of information interviewing is simple: to help you learn more about a job or organisation. It's not a backdoor route into providing you with an unfair advantage in an interview; nor is it an alternative way for canvassing for a job.

Information interviewing is based on four key assumptions.

1. If you want to find out about a job or an organisation, you can't do better than to talk to someone who is currently employed in that job or organisation.

2. The majority of people are (within reason) usually only too happy to discuss their careers, jobs or organisations with others, and often find the experience of talking about them quite pleasant.

3. Most people (within reason) are prepared to spare 20 minutes to help others in their search for a career.

4. Most people with jobs know of other jobs that are about to come up.

Getting started

Like networking, information interviewing approximates to normal human behaviour. This is partly why it is so effective. But don't let this lull you into a false sense of security. It only works if you abide by the following 'rules'.

- Only contact people at a level appropriate to your skills and experience. In other words, instead of trying to speak to the chief executive, aim to meet with someone who has recently entered the organisation, or who is working in a job appropriate to your level.

- When contacting them, ask for no more than 20 minutes. Never 'half an hour' because it sounds too general and vague. Twenty minutes; no more, no less.

- Remember: the aim of information interviewing is to find out more about a job in which you may or may not be interested. It's a unique and powerful chance to find out if this really is the job for you. It isn't a sneaky, backdoor way to asking for a job. This is cheating and will not reflect well on you.

- Information Interviewing is all about *research*. Be ready to use the 'R' word when asking your contact for an interview.

- When setting up an information interview, personal recommendations and introductions are worth far more than speculative letters or phone calls. In this connection, if possible, avoid HR departments and various personal assistants – most of whom are highly skilled in sniffing out potential job searchers and terminating any 'unorthodox' approaches to their organisations.

- When you arrive for an information interview (and remember, it will be held at a time, date and venue convenient to your contact, not to you) be sure to have with you a list of questions – real questions, questions that you genuinely require answers to. And on no occasion should any of your questions include 'Please may I have a job?'

- Important point: before the interview finishes, always be sure to ask: 'Who, in your opinion, should I go and speak to now?' This question is essential because, once your contact ('Contact A') suggests a name to you, you can then contact that person ('Contact B') with opener, '*Hello Ms Jones, Mr X has suggested that I speak to you ...*'. Once you are able to begin conversations in such a manner, you'll never have to cold call again. From now on in, you're an insider!

- Always, immediately after an information interview, write a letter of thanks to your contact. Handwritten letters carry maximum impression value. If your contact has told you to stay in touch, do so.

Information interviewing is definitely not rocket science. But it works, as long as you keep to the rules and respect the integrity and professional positions of your contacts. Some organisations have an automatic ban on any unconventional approaches by prospective job seekers; others don't. Before making any approach to an organisation or person, do your homework carefully.

Using information interviewing has one major advantage: it puts you in charge of your own career – a key consideration for most graduates, given the levels of competition in today's job market. Once you've become familiar with its conventions and have developed your own style, you'll be amazed at how soon information interviewing will take you to job leads of the kind that you didn't know existed.

Better still, by uncovering your own job leads, you'll find that you are the only candidate.

"I think and think for months and years. Ninety-nine times, the conclusion is false. The hundredth time I am right."

Albert Einstein

E = Employability, Q = Qualifications, WE = Work Experience, S = Strategies and C = Contacts

Conclusion

$$E = Q + WE + S \times C$$

What E = Q + WE + S x C tells you about the new world of work

This book is based on an assumption and a formula.

The assumption is: thanks to rising student numbers and the impact of the credit crunch, the world of graduate careers has changed – probably for good.

The formula, E = Q + WE + S x C, argues that to be employable in this new world of work, you need a range of components.

First, you need a degree; but as we have seen, when it comes to the job market, not all degrees can offer you the same opportunity to achieve a graduate-level job. And it's not just degrees; *where* you choose to study for your degree is becoming an increasingly important consideration.

Second, you definitely need work experience. In all degree subjects, work experience (increasingly referred to as 'internship') is what makes all the difference. Before you choose your degree, make sure that you ask how your prospective university plans to ensure that you have plenty of opportunities to gain relevant work experience. Best of all, look for courses that have work experience built into the academic programme.

Third, you need the strategies, skills and knowledge to know how to market yourself to employers. Work experience and qualifications by themselves aren't enough if you don't know how to package them to employers.

Fourth – and arguably most important of all – you need contacts. Contacts, in this new world of work, are the key. You gain them, ideally, via work experience – although your university tutors and careers advisers will be able to help you begin to network. Contacts are the difference between being almost there and being able to achieve your goals.

> **Together, qualifications, work experience, skills and contacts are the key to graduate employability.**

Increasingly, as author Charles Ledbeatter has argued, this means learning to operate in the 'thin air' economy of services rather than products. Things that exist in your mind, not things you can drop on your foot. The value of Microsoft is six and a half times that of General Motors, even though GM employs more people, makes more products and owns more factories. In fact, the biggest employer in the world today, Wal-Mart, doesn't actually make anything at all – it sells things. In a world of technology, global communications and services, if you can touch something, it's probably not worth that much. The *big* money lies in ideas, transactions, emotions and brands. It's all about being *unique*.

Five steps to taking control

Below are five steps which, if you apply them, will help you to begin the process of taking control of your graduate career.

Step 1: Know the competition

As we have seen, there are currently 2.4 million students at UK universities. Being a student is the most popular occupation in the world. In Britain, one in three 18-year-olds now opt to study for a degree (the eventual target is one in two).

The expansion of higher education over the past decade has been nothing short of revolutionary. However, when it comes to employment, things are not so straightforward.

Nevertheless, as more people emerge from university, it is clear that no one can be complacent. Like it or not, when you graduate you are going to be in direct competition with more graduates, from more universities, possessing more qualifications than ever before!

Step 2: Never make a permanent career decision

'What do you want to do when you graduate?'

How often are you asked that question? Choosing a career – and then sticking to that choice – was once sound advice. Not anymore. Work is evolving so rapidly that many of today's students will eventually work in jobs that have not yet been invented. A strange thought perhaps, but who, 20 years ago, would have

> Who would have thought that Lehman Brothers, a 160-year old investment bank, would vanish in just one day?

predicted how many jobs would be created by the internet? Or lost to inventions such as the ATM (cash point), which alone has led to the disappearance of up to 300,000 banking jobs?

Unfortunately, one unavoidable by-product of living in fast-moving times is that exact planning – particularly career planning – is all but impossible. Flexibility, contingency plans, alternative strategies are the order of the day. The next time someone asks you what you want to do after graduation, tell them your ideal job hasn't been invented yet.

Step 3: Blame nobody, expect no lucky breaks – just make sure you do something

According to one academic study, there are essentially two kinds of job hunters: *purists* and *players*. *Purists* believe that job markets are inherently fair and meritocratic; that one day all their hard work, qualifications and quiet dedication will be recognised and rewarded; that keeping their head down is the best way to get ahead.

Players, on the other hand, approach job hunting like playing a game: there are rules, tactics and opponents. They accept that job markets are unfair; that ultimately, the odds are stacked in certain people's favour. The object of the *player's* game is to overturn those odds by using all their skills, experience, contacts, motivation and sheer guts. *Purists* wait for opportunities to emerge. *Players* go out and create them. Guess which are best placed to take advantage of today's job market? Which are you?

Step 4: Expect fantastic opportunities to arise

Everyone has their dreams and ambitions. Some want to be highly successful in business; others harbour secret desires to be film stars, models, footballers, politicians. For many, these dreams remain just that — dreams. Yet for some people, such dreams do become reality. Psychologist Richard Wiseman argues that

> The next time someone asks you what you want to do after graduation, tell them your ideal job hasn't been invented yet.

people who achieve their career objectives often apply four principles, consciously or subconsciously:

1. They actively maximise their exposure to 'chance' opportunities. In other words, they search out and take small steps which lead them out of their comfort zone.

2. Rather than over-rationalising things, successful people tend to listen to their hunches and are quite prepared to follow their initiative.

3. They expect good things to happen to them. This allows them to approach new situations, such as joining a new class, positively and with enthusiasm.

4. They have mastered the art of bouncing back from pitfalls, often managing to turn setbacks into new opportunities.

Remember, Thomas Edison took out 99 patents on the light bulb before finally settling on a winning design. Rather than conceding defeat, he argued that the light bulb was an invention in 100 steps!

Step 5: Claim your vision – *now!*

Most people devote more time to planning their holidays than they do to planning their careers. But not you! Your career is too important to be left to the forces of chance. Altogether, you have just 1,000 days at university, and, if you use them wisely, in career terms they can be the most important 1,000 days of your life.

What to do if you *still* don't know what to do

As this book has shown, few potentially life-changing decisions are as important as career decisions. Few, decisions, however, are taken so lightly.

But it doesn't have to be like that. Today's job market calls for a revolution in the way that we think about and make career decisions. Being undecided about your career while you're a student is no bad thing; certainly, it's much better than making an impulsive choice that might cost you years to remedy. And there's another reason why you shouldn't be in any hurry to make up your mind. Organisations are changing so rapidly that the chances are that your 'ideal' job has not yet been invented. Many of today's students will, in the next few years, find themselves working for organisations that don't yet exist, selling products and services that we currently have no idea that we need. The fact is, keeping your options open is better than closing them down.

Below are ten steps you can take now to start getting your career into gear.

Tune in to your passions!

Step one is to change the way you think and talk about careers. When it comes to choosing how you want to spend your one, unique life, you need to

> **" Choose a job you like and you'll never work a day in your life. "**
>
> Confucius

ditch half-hearted terminology and tune in to your passions – the things about which you're passionate and excited about, that motivate you ... or that you're simply curious to find out more about.

Focus on your skills

Make a list of your skills – the things that you are good at. It sounds obvious, but it's usually tougher to do than it seems. Ask yourself this: *'What are the things that I can do that others can't?'* For a second opinion, talk to friends and family.

Location, location, location

Career options are also shaped by practical considerations, such as where you want to work, and how far from home you'd be prepared to travel. Is relocation an option? How you answer this will have an impact on your choice of career. Think about it carefully.

Don't be a 'wash 'n' go' student

Remember that studying at university offers multiple chances to develop and acquire many personal and social skills – skills that are suitable for many careers. Don't leave it until your final year to begin planning your career.

Make sure it's your future we're talking about

Deep down, many people's career ideas are a reflection of the influence of other people – parents, teachers, lecturers, even careers advisers. Breaking free of these influences can be difficult, but ultimately it's essential – this is your life we're talking about, right?

Take steps to move out of your comfort zone

Try not to be afraid of taking risks. Stepping outside of your comfort zone is a crucial career attitude. If your degree subject doesn't point to a particular career, make sure that you use your time at university to gain work experience so that you can explore different fields and sectors.

It's good to talk

Seek out good advice. Careers advice, before, during and after university, is essential for everyone. Careers advisers are equipped with a superb range of skills, expertise, information and advice. Use them!

Lists are for wimps!

Everyone, at some time or other, has found themselves hoping that someone, somewhere has a secret list of tips which fits their own personal qualifications and skills. If this is you, brace yourself: *there is not, and never has been any such list*. Career opportunities for graduates have never been more varied or exciting. But to work out which is the best career for you, you'll have to do your homework.

Your job is not your career

Never confuse the terms 'job' and 'career'. Avoid using the two inter-changeably. What's the difference? You can be sacked from a job, but you can't be sacked from a career. Instead, your career is your lifetime's project, it's what you do and it's what gets you out of bed in the morning. Most of all, a career should be fun. A job pays the bills.

Being in a lousy job isn't your fault – staying in one is

Following on from this, it's perfectly acceptable to start work in a 'job' that, although on the surface it looks like a no-hoper, provides you with the opportunities to acquire new skills, contacts, ideas and money. Most graduates change jobs several times in the first few years after university. So worry less about the sort of job in which you begin your life after university. Only start worrying if it looks like you're going to be trapped there.

Last point

Before embarking on your journey of career discovery, try Prospects Planner – an on-line career education programme designed to help you work out your interests, desires, ambitions and goals, before matching you to a series of graduate-related occupations. Prospects Planner is available at www.prospects.ac.uk.

The formula checklist

To help you assess how prepared you are for the new world of graduate work, see how far you get with the following checklist.

Q = Qualifications (Section 2)

☐ Am I clear about the careers options available to me with my degree subject?

☐ Have I checked what graduates from this subject do after graduation?

☐ Do I know how my subject compares to others in its subject field?

☐ Does my university have a strong track record for employability?

☐ Has my university got an Employability Strategy? If so, have I read it?

☐ Have I met with my tutors and careers advisers to discuss my career plans?

☐ Does my degree course offer me the possibility of choosing various employability options, eg work-related modules, employer-based dissertations?

☐ As part of my degree course, are there opportunities to record my career-related learning?

☐ Have I considered a range of universities – and do I know what employability is like at my preferred university?

WE = Work experience (Section 3)

☐ To date, do I consider my work experience to be above average?

☐ Does my degree subject offer me the chance to opt for work experience placements or internships?

☐ Do I take every opportunity to increase my awareness of the world of work?

☐ Have I got a part-time job?

☐ Do I plan my summer vacation to ensure that I gain experience of new types of work?

☐ Am I able to offer future employers a range of additional skills and experiences?

☐ Have I gained recent and relevant work experience in my chosen field?

S = Strategies (Section 4)

☐ Is my CV up to date? Have I had it checked by a careers adviser?

☐ Have I arranged to meet with my careers adviser or tutor to discuss my plans?

☐ Am I aware of what employment rates are like for my chosen career?

☐ Do I have plans to attend university open days?

☐ Do I have the skills to write convincing applications?

- ☐ Have I had an interview in the past year?
- ☐ Do I have a range of interesting extracurricular interests that I could talk to employers about?
- ☐ Can I make a list of my top five transferable skills?
- ☐ Is my writing style good enough to impress employers?

C = Contacts (Section 5)

- ☐ Do I have contacts whom I could approach to help me with my career search?
- ☐ Do these contacts know what I want to do after university?
- ☐ Am I constantly looking for opportunities to build my network of contacts?
- ☐ Have I got a business card?
- ☐ Do I have a mentor – someone I can turn to for advice and support?

Case study: Bashir Mohammed

Job title: **Area Manager**
Business area: **Rental**
Year joined: **2000**

Hello Bashir. Tell us about your worst nightmare.

My worst nightmare would be finding myself stuck in a dead end job, doing the same thing all day every day, and never seeing any career progression. Thankfully, Enterprise is nothing like that. Being in control of your career is a reality here. What's more, every employee starts in the same position as senior management did when they first began – so I knew if I worked hard I'd be able to find exactly the same kind of success as them.

In fact, one of the main reasons why the Enterprise graduate training scheme was so appealing to me was the clear career progression path it offered. Alongside that, it empowered me to look after a £million+ business, take genuine ownership, and make the type of tough decisions that come with running a business. Finally, my "work hard, play hard" mentality meant I felt assured that if I did well, I'd reap the benefits long term.

It's fair to say I've done what I set out to do. In 2005, I was promoted to National Account Manager, looking after approximately £12 million worth of corporate business for the UK. During this time, I was also involved in some very high level relationship building with various companies. After successfully negotiating contracts with these companies for a further two years, I was asked to look after the entire central region.

To sum things up, I'd say if you work hard and enjoy what you do, you'll succeed at Enterprise. Every day is a new day here, and although it's been said before (and will probably be said again) you really *do* get out what you put in. I couldn't ask for more.

Enterprise Rent-A-Car: Company Profile

Enterprise Rent-A-Car
At Enterprise, we combine the opportunities of a huge, internationally successful car rental company with a more personal, entrepreneurial approach that lets individuals stand out. That's because we're divided up into hundreds of smaller businesses (or branches), which you'll form part of and learn how to run yourself.

Our training scheme
You'll start off as a Management Trainee, and after an initial classroom-based orientation session you'll be assigned to a branch office for the hands-on business training. This includes management skills, finance, marketing, operations, sales and customer service, giving you the kind of business knowledge you'd only usually get from an MBA. Within a year you could be promoted to Assistant Manager. From then on, you'll also receive a percentage of the profits generated by your own branch, which means you could earn more thanks to our performance-based culture.

Our career progression
Throughout the scheme, there's a series of carefully monitored tests and evaluations, after which you'll receive pay increases, rewards and more opportunities for promotion, working your way up to Branch Manager, then Area Manager, City Manager and beyond. You'll also have the opportunity to specialise if you find an area of the business you're particularly interested in.

Our background
Enterprise started in the US in 1957 and we now have a turnover of $10.1 billion, employing more than 66,000 people across the UK, Ireland, Germany, the USA and Canada, with over 3,400 in the UK and over 190 in Ireland. We've won more than a few awards in our time too. Most recently, we were voted as one of the 'best places to launch a career' by Business Week, and featured in 'The Times Top 50 Where Women Want To Work'.

All about you
Join us and you can take advantage of enormous earning potential, a truly entrepreneurial environment, and a commitment to having fun, that few if any other companies can offer. If you have the potential to be a good leader, with strong negotiation skills and a high degree of self-motivation, then you'll almost certainly love working here.

To find out more, please visit www.enterprisealive.co.uk/gjf2010

Glossary

AGR	The Association of Graduate Recruiters – an organisation that represents leading graduate recruiters.
AGCAS	The Association of Graduate Careers Advisory Services – represents the vast majority of UK university careers services.
blue-chip	A large and wealthy organisation – usually one quoted on the stock market.
DLHE	The Destinations of Leavers from Higher Education survey – a comprehensive survey undertaken by all universities every winter on behalf of HESA. DLHE data forms the basis of university employability league tables.
first destinations	The first 'destination' that a graduate is recorded as going to within six months of graduation, when the DLHE survey is taken by HESA.
HESA	The Higher Education Statistical Agency – the government body that undertakes the DHLE survey.
milk round	An old-fashioned term to describe the process whereby graduate recruiters visit university campuses, usually in the first semester, to hold a series of recruitment events and interviews. Although the milk round no longer formally exists at some universities, employers still hold a series of events, usually in the first semester.
recruiter	An employer or an employer's representative whose job involves recruiting graduates

Websites

Association of Graduate Careers Advisory Services: www.agcas.org.uk
Business Link: www.businesslink.gov.uk
Global Management Challenge: www.worldgmc.com
Graduate Prospects: www.prospects.ac.uk
High Fliers: www.highfliers.co.uk
Regional Development Agencies: www.englandsrdas.com

Further reading

59 Seconds: Think a little, change a lot, Richard Wiseman (Macmillan)

The AGR Graduate Recruitment Survey 2009, Association of Graduate Recruiters (Warwick)

Destinations of Leavers from Higher Education Institutions, 2007-08, Higher Education Statistics Agency

Living on thin air: the new economy, Charles Ledbeatter (Penguin)

Screw it, let's do it, Lessons in life, Richard Branson (Virgin Books)

The Seven Benefits of Hiring Graduates, Graduate Recruitment Bureau

Seven Years On, Peter Elias and Kate Purcell

What do graduates do? AGCAS (2010)

Why work experience matters! Real Prospects 2009 graduates' experiences of placements, internships and work experience, Kathrine Jensen (2009).

Practise & Pass Professional: Numeracy Tests, Alan Redman (Trotman)

Practise & Pass Professional: Verbal Reasoning Tests, Alan Redman (Trotman)

What Can I do with An Arts Degree, Gill Sharp and Beryl Dixon (Trotman)

You're Hired! CV, Corinne Mills (Trotman)

You're Hired! Interview, Judi James (Trotman)

You're Hired! Interview Answers, Ceri Roderick and Stephen Lucks (Trotman)

You're Hired! Psychometric Tests, Ceri Roderick and James Meachin (Trotman)

Occupational change and the expansion of Higher Education in the UK: the impact on graduate earnings Paper presented at the International Conference on the Development of Competencies in the World of Work and Education, Ljubljana, 23-26 September 2009. Elias, P. and K. Purcell (2009)

Is mass higher education working? Evidence from the labour market experiences of recent graduates National Institute Economic review No. 190, October 2004, pp.60-74. Elias, P. and K. Purcell (2004)